WATERLILLY

Once Upon a Soul: *My Awakening*

I let myself drift until I could drift no more and my mind became like mirrors within mirrors. The memories I'd forgotten and the thoughts I'd misplaced bombarded me throughout this awakening. I've often wondered where my dreams have hidden over these blank spaces referred to as years. Sometimes I find myself conjuring up old conversations while remembering my forgotten past. I think it was the summer of my thirteenth year when I went through what is commonly known as a "*depression*". Not that this was any different than any other time I have been depressed, but this was my first. At the time I didn't know what it meant to be depressed. Everything around me seemed alien and I thought the only solution was to withdraw and escape the world by putting on a set of headphones and blasting the music. That was then. This is now and I don't have any headphones but am experiencing the same feelings. However, instead of withdrawing into myself I prefer to brood over the fact that the world is sick, myself included.

Through most of the day my good feelings are backed up by ones of anger and frustration. I feel abandoned, I feel alone. I tell everyone that once I put my mind to something it always gets done. What they fail to realize is my mind hasn't been set on anything.

From a very young age my right foot has always been in front of my left foot, a never ending, full steam ahead approach to life with my good foot leading whilst forgetting my bad foot trailed close behind. I've always felt pushed into independence. It was the influence of my mother that inadvertently placed my feet and unbeknownst to me this would be the one thing that helped me through the most difficult situations.... one step at a time, one in front of the other. I like everyone else am the product of my environment. That is why I decided to enroll in a brush-up course on how to walk through life on "*both feet*". My own "*Do-It-Yourself Become a Better Person*" course I thought would take all of three years (maximum) to finish with at least an "*A*". It is twenty years later and I haven't even taken the first quiz yet.

It is so difficult to become more humane when my environment is filled with people who aren't people anymore. As I see it the problem doesn't begin with society. It stems from the individual. Why are we so afraid? Why the different mask for each occasion? People fear the unknown. If everyone became aware of the unknown they would be confronted with death. The death they live, the death they share with friends, the death they call love. If only they could see that the world within is far more tragic than the world without. Universal problem solving starts with changing oneself. Not the one next to, above us, or behind us.

Sometimes while watching the scenes of my multiple selves, I wonder how is it possible to have lived so many lives simultaneously. I have never regretted my many rebirths. It is amazing to discover and rediscover that the waterlily within my soul still blooms and is immortal. This possession will never be taken from me. My waterlily wills me to continue on forever.

What about the dandelions, those ever so beautiful flowers that become weeds. They surround my blossom and every so often I have to clear away a lot of shit before I am able to find the Divine's ultimate center of beauty. Over the years I have written poetry, written stories and wept until there were no more tears. My eyes heal, my ears control and my mind journeys within the horizon of happiness, solutions and everlasting life. I no longer feel the anger of frustration, I feel the pain of humanity. I no longer have scars, I have open wounds. Which I dress daily with love, faith, endurance and strength. Knowing that with each birth my pain and wounds will become pools of wisdom, truth, understanding and solutions for others to bathe in so they too can be resurrected from the death they once lived.

After each awakening I wonder where my dreams will float, where my poetry will live? Where will my next rebirth take me on Jacob's ladder. One day I will find out but until that time I will make a life for others with the being of my soul, with the soul of my being!

Chapter I

THE EARLY YEARS

My father is African American and my mother is Dutch. He at the time of my birth was a musician and apparently came to Israel looking for his roots. My mother was born in Holland and a holocaust survivor. She came to Israel as a new immigrant. They lived in Israel until I was 11 months old then moved to Europe. We lived in Holland, Germany and Luxemburg. My sister was born in Holland in 1965. In 1969 we moved to America where my brother and youngest sister were born. I have dual citizenship being both American and Israeli. I was raised between these 4 worlds if you include the European and the African elements of my family.

They met at a jazz concert in Haifa in the Mother Garden. There was only one seat left and it happened to be next to my mother. Afterwards they went out. Mom thought Dad was arrogant and self centered. Well…whatever happened happened, they continued to see one another. Mom got pregnant. At the time inter-religious marriages were not possible in Israel so they got married in cypress. . I was born in Eilat when there was only one hotel and 800 inhabitants. Dad along with a partner started the first scuba diving school.

In 1969 we moved to America because my grandmother (dad's mother) had several strokes, she was paralyzed and wasn't expected to make it. She ended up outliving my grandfather by 11 years who had catered to her every need.

We lived in NE Philadelphia. It was my first time being around black people other than my father. I have very fond memories of my grandfather, a gentle man, very quiet, very calm. The first night we arrived in America we needed police assistance to open the door to my grandparents home. Grandpa had fallen asleep and couldn't hear us. Grandma was still in the hospital. The next day we went to visit her.

I was horrified and petrified; she looked deformed because of the stroke. I refused to get close to her. I was too scared. I didn't want to kiss her either much to my parent's embarrassment. We lived with them for one year. I went to nursery school in Philadelphia. Dad studied at Temple University. After a year we moved to Levittown, a steel workers town. I went to George Washington elementary school. I was a good student.

My childhood was not a happy one. Many times I wanted to run away. I remember visiting a girlfriend after school. A few minutes after I arrived at her house I crouched up in a corner of her bedroom with my back to everyone and cried uncontrollably.

She ran to get her parents. Her family came in the room and tried to calm me down. I remember not being able to stop crying and not being able to move from that spot. I didn't want to go home. Finally one of her uncles talked to me softly and kindly, I stopped crying. Eventually I got it together enough to be able to go home.

By about the 4th grade my teachers wanted move me up a grade. My father refused. He said I was not emotionally ready. I was so hurt. I wanted to move on, to advance, to feel good about myself, proud of myself. I felt he was holding me back. . *Emotonally not ready* – huh. I guess not – he had been fucking around with my emotions since I could remember– he was good at that.

One day I ran away. Packed some cookies went up the road, stayed a while by the creek, just wandered around, trying to figure out where to go, anywhere so that I wouldn't have to go back. In the end I returned home. I came in the house – mom hadn't noticed I was gone. When I told her I ran away she told me I should have stayed longer… So much for my great escape.

Very often, in fact regularly I remember waking up in the middle of the night and finding myself in the dark in the front room. It felt as if I was being called to the front room while I was asleep. My father was always there, always naked. There were other times that he would "play" with me – but it didn't feel right. I shut down. I created a world for myself that was governed by selective memory. I consciously and subconsciously chose what was real and what wasn't real.

Daddy... why?! Whyyyyyyyyyy?! Why do you hate me? Why do you hurt me ALL of the time? Why does my heart hurt? Why does my soul hurt? Why does my body hurt? Why does my "stuff" hurt to the point of horrible pain ALL of the time? I want to die! I want to disappear! I want to be invisible so that you can't see me anymore! Maybe if I don't exist the pain will stop. Maybe if I disappear the fear and horror will disappear too! I want to die but at the same time I am afraid of death.

I can picture myself dead... just a small body of mist in outer space in the darkness. And it is this darkness and this mist of nothingness that has me so afraid that I can't think, I can't move, I can't function. Then I wake up from this "*dream*" and bring the fear, the horror, and the pain with me into daylight.

Most of me hates you! But the part I am so ashamed of is the part that loves you, the part that has gotten so used to the pain, fear and horror that it excites me. It has even become erotic. I am so ashamed. Eventually I looked forward to being turned on even at my young age of 7 or 8 or 9 or 10 or 11. I am ashamed because I know in my soul this isn't right, it's evil, it's shameful. I am ashamed because you changed me. And then you blamed it all on me. You blamed everything on me. You blamed your relationship with mom on me. You blamed the divorce on me. You blamed my body on me.

Everyday you made sure to tell me that I was *UGLY, NOT HUMAN AND DIDN'T DESERVE TO EXIST ON THIS EARTH.* And everyday I looked in the mirror and believed it. Everyday I looked in the mirror and felt shame!

Meals eaten at the table, became the "*LET'S MAKE FUN OF AND HUMILIATE LLYANA*" show. Dinner time was always traumatic. Dad always found ways to humiliate and make fun of me in front of everyone. He made fun of my body. Statements like, "*When your breasts finally get big we won't have to buy any more milk we can use yours*", were the norm. Everyone thought it was hilarious. I was defenseless, and you included the whole family. They all laughed at me and thought it was funny. Let's make fun of my breasts because I started puberty early. Let's make fun of my body. But worst of all.... the more I sat there with my head down and cried, the more you made fun of me and the more everyone else laughed. Humiliation and shame is what I am, is what I will always be, is what I am destined to be. I am the but of everyone's jokes so I must be a joke.

I wake up in the middle of the night, almost every night, as if I am under a spell, and am drawn to the living room, where you are sitting in the dark, in the middle of the floor completely naked. It goes blank after that and somehow someway I end up back in my bed. Did I blank out from the pain, from the humiliation? Did I blank out from the shame of being turned out by you? Or did I blank out from the horror of the "ritual" I was unwillingly led into? Did I blank out because orgasm was the only thing that relieved my pain, and I am ashamed because I don't even know what that is.

Death follows me everywhere. I fall apart and become hysterical because I live, breath and wear death like I wear your smell when you are finished with me. Then when you are finished with me and the night is over and daylight comes you start over again and I feel doomed. You even made a sign for me to wear around my neck with "NOT HUMAN" written on it as a reminder to what I am not and what I will never be.

You even kept me from going up a grade because you said I wasn't emotionally ready. I waited at home so excited, so proud of myself that finally I had the chance to be awesome. Finally I am not the piece of shit you lead me to believe I am. You and mom came home from the meeting at school. I was smiling from ear to ear, so excited to hear the good news. Finally you told me it was not going to happen. You told the teachers no, because I was not emotionally ready. My whole world fell apart!!!!!! I will never get out of this. I will never get ahead. I will never leave this shit.

I want to hate you. I want to be angry but I don't know how. The only thing I feel is shame. I even feel shame for how my body feels when I am with you. I feel shame because I have no control. I feel shame because no one loves me enough to protect me from this, from you. In my mind I hate the feel of your touch, but my body feels differently. In my mind I hate the thought of your "thing" close to me, on me, near me, on top of me, but my body feels differently. In my mind I hate the thought of your tongue.... but my body feels differently. And I am so so lost not having control over my body. I am so ashamed that I don't know how to hate you or be angry with you because my body feels differently. I am so ashamed that I don;t have the strength or know how to make you stop. Because in my mind I know what you're doing is evil..... but my body feels differently.

It's like you cast a spell on me or you cursed me to not be able to say no... to not have the strength to make it stop.... to not have the courage to fight you... to not have a life where you didn't exist. I am nothing but your rag doll, your twisted rag doll whose mind and soul say one thing but whose body says something else. Why are you doing this to me? Was I put here on this earth just for you? I have no escape, I have no where to go, no where to run to, no where to hide, no where to be just me, no where to be just happy.

I wish I could hate you. I wish I could be angry..... but all I feel is shame, fear, panic and doom. I am consumed by doom and shame. I don't want to be here, I don't want to exist anymore, I don't want to live this life anymore.... but most of all..... I wish I could hate you!

One time at breakfast, my sister told him she dreamt he had raped her. My heart stopped. I was afraid to move. He very matter of factly stated this was perfectly normal... "*According to psychologists, all girls at one stage or another dream of their fathers raping them and for her not to worry. In fact if a girl didn't dream her father raped her this would be cause for concern*"... I was only 9 or 10 at the time but I was disgusted, I was horrified. In my soul I knew this was wrong. In that moment I vowed I would never dream about my father. Thirty some years later, I never have.

On a Saturday morning, I was sitting in the front room, he was in the kitchen. I walked into the kitchen and saw raw ground meat all over the floor. He told me he was angry with mom, pretended the meat was her, he tore her apart and threw her all over the kitchen floor. Therefore from a very early age I felt I had to protect my mother. I was always concerned about her and never wanted to make any waves or problems. Dad was physically and verbally abusive. I felt I had to be her guardian and protector. She confided in me a quite a bit. There were problems and I did get into trouble, but in my soul, in my heart I tried not to burden my mother with my shit.

We didn't have a lot of money so when mom started the divorce proceedings, we did not move out of the house. She slept in the room with my sister and I. One night dad barged into our bedroom, snatched mom out of my bed and said her place was in the bed with him. I was so scared. Mom refused to go. She placed her handbag in the room and told us to be ready. I wanted her to grab her bags, and us and get out. Run away from it all. She continued to refuse to go into the bedroom with dad and stayed in bed with me. He told her she had a certain amount of time to get out of my bed and into his or else. I told her I was afraid that if he didn't get "*it*" from her he would try to get "*it*" from me. She immediately got up and went into the room with him. I could hear him having sex with her – it made me sick to my stomach. I always wished she would have taken us and left so I wouldn't have to hear that mess.

My father beat me for using too much toilet paper. What the hell did I know, I just wanted to wipe my ass. I was only allowed to use one square for #1 and two squares for #2. I have a thing about toilet tissue to this day. I use lots and lots of toilet tissue. You would think that I have a hippo ass. I do this to spite my father.

There was a private room in the house. One which we were forbidden to enter on penalty of death or so we believed. He spent time in the room with the door locked. Curious person that I am I had to see what was in the room. I picked the lock. I didn't understand what it was all about, I just knew mom had to see. She was afraid dad would find out. I insisted. I picked the lock again, we went inside…there was a skull and bones on the shelf, candles, a ring of salt in the middle of the floor, with a five – pointed star and other unfamiliar things on the shelves. All of which I know today as occult paraphanalia. Mom stood there with her mouth open. We closed the door and didn't speak about it again.

When we eventually moved away from dad and out of the house, she received an envelope in the mail with burnt ashes in it. We immediately knew it was from him. Mom, my sister and I along with a friend of mom's, and her 2 daughters stood in a circle all touching the envelope and giving it good energy, positive energy, love energy.

The letter was sent back. Whenever I visited him I brought in his mail. A few days after returning the envelope with the burnt ashes, I brought the mail in as usual. I recognized the letter with the ashes. My heart skipped a beat. I thought about putting it back, but my dad would know I was aware of what was going on. I brought it in with the rest of the mail and played the nut role, as if I knew nothting. He singled out this particular letter. I was sweating bullets. He said the letter had to be from mom and why would she send him something like that. He hadn't even opened the letter, how would he know what was inside if he hadn't sent it in the first place?

He was also a walking talking genius. He played at least four to five instruments. I have seen him pick up an instrument for the first time and after playing around with it for a few minutes he would successfully manage to get some kind of music from it. He spoke English, French, Hebrew, German and Dutch fluently. He could sing, knew the Bible like the back of his hand and had a lot of knowledge on several other subjects.

The one good thing that did come out of my relationship with dad was intellect. My quest and thirst for knowledge. Many a night I would stay up late and have wonderful conversations with him on numerous subjects.

From the age of four, every Friday he would come home with a surprise for my sister and I. It was always the same thing. A book for each one of us. It was the highlight of my week. By the time I was eleven years old I was reading highschool and college level books. It was my escape from one reality to another. I inhaled books. Around the same time I thought a lot about life and especially about death. I was petrified! I would lay in the bed at night and could picture myself dead. A thin vapor floating amonst the stars alone in the dark.

A fear would come over me from inside of my stomach. I couldn't breath, I became hysterical crying and panicked. My parents tried everything to calm me down, to give me some kind of solace. Deep breathing exercises and creative visualizations. Dad was into pyramids. He tried placing one over me. Nothng worked. Finally mom brought me several books about reincarnation, about psychology – whatever she could find. Nothing worked. Finally one day dad told me a lot of people find answers reading the Bible. He gave me his copy of the New Testament, I read it cover to cover.

In Revelations the 12th chapter I found a scripture referring to the 144,000 saints that would never die. They were saviors of the world and acquired everlasting life. From that day forward I prayed diligently to be in this number. And so began my sincere quest in search of God. I always believed in a higher power but didn't know what it was or how to get to it. I always wanted to be a part of God but didn't know what that meant. This scripture gave me a direction to go in and gave me hope.

Another escape for me was nature. The sunsets, the rain, the grass and the trees. To this day I am a tree hugger. I would sit for hours on our front porch at night and watch the rain, smell it, feel the wind, enjoy the sound. At some point I would become the rain, become the sunset, I was the trees and the wind.

I saw a movie a few years ago with Anothy Hopkins, Donald Sutherland and Cuba Gooding Jr., "*Betrayed*". About a man, (Anthony Hopkins) who was an anthropologist studying gorillas in Africa. Every time he returned to Africa he would stay longer and longer in the bush until one day he never returned.

There is a scene in this movie wherein he had been with the gorillas for a while. They were used to him being around. It started to rain, the gorillas continued on about their business as usual, sitting around, eating leaves. While Anthony Hopkins was trying to protect himself from the rain using a large banana leaf. He looked around after being unsuccessful at keeping dry, and realized how the gorillas were unaffected. He put the leaf down, looked up at the sky, let the rain fall on his face, lifted his hands toward the rain and at the moment, in that very instant he was perfectly free, perfectly in tune with the creations and purely elated.

This is me. This is the purity of heart I feel in the rain, next to a tree, in a meadow of flowers, at one with the sunset, the clouds, the heavens and the earth. There is no death in these moments, no pain, no suffering, no darkness. Only life, only eternity, only the natural life giving cycles of the universe. This was my quest. The 12th chapter of Revelations not only gave me hope, it opened up a door within me that gave me a glimpse of what happiness and eternity could be.

As time went on these glimpses dimmed. My prayers continued

but I still felt lost, still felt I didn't belong. I finally had enough. I climbed into the tree in the front yard and asked my sister to get me a knife because I wanted to kill myself. As afraid and petrified as I was of death, I was going to kill myself... go figure! Mom came out, I went into the house, by then I was hysterical. She slapped me to calm me down. She called dad. Not long after that I went into counseling.

At some point I overheard a conversation mom had with one of her friends about artificial insemination. A light bulb went off. I could have a baby without having to be with a man?!. I would have some one to love and some one who loved me. Yeah right, when I asked mom about it she thought I was just being nosy. Maybe I was, it didn't matter though. I had so much love to give I could give it to my children. I wanted a lot of children, but soon came to the conclusion that I didn't want to bring children into this world just so they could grow up and die. Therefore I decided to get my tubes tied. Or so I thought at the very experienced and wise age of twelve.

Three months before my twelfth birthday, at 5am, I woke up to my mother crying and pleading with my father. It sounded as if he was hitting her. I paced back and forth not sure what to do, scared to death to do the wrong thing and reap my father's wrath. I woke my sister up. Asked her to watch my back while I snuck into the dining room in order to call the police. I reached out to pick up the phone and stopped in my tracks. What if dad picked up the other end and heard my voice? So we both left the house going door to door hoping some one would hear us. Up and down the street. No one answered. A neighbor across the street finally opened her door. By then I was crying, I asked her to call the police. Ten minutes later the police arrived. I stepped outside to meet them. Suddenly we heard glass shattering and my mother screaming out of the bathroom window. She had locked herself in the bathroom and broke the window with her hand. *"Help me, some one please help me. He is trying to kill me"*.

The police ran up to the house, one of the officers held me back. My father answered the door, all nonchalant. My mother flew out and I went in. Dad was a sight. His hair was in disarray, he looked pitiful. I remember actually feeling sorry for him. The police advised my mother to move out – going through a divorce and living in the same house is not a good idea. She had no money and nowhere to go. A close friend said we could stay at her house. Mom didn't press charges. I wasn't staying with dad and neither was my sister. Dad refused to let mom take my two youngest siblings , they were ages five and six. The policemen stated they couldn't get involved. Mom had to go. My sister and I went with her.

I CRIED IN DECEMBER

I cried in December, patiently waiting, holding on, till the appointed time. Season after season of emotion choreographed within the theater of my soul. Pirouette alongside pirouette before an audience of pain, suggesting the onslaught of repeated debuts.

Woe to the warrior dancing upon the arena of hope, Existing only to negotiate the reprieve of an age gone by. Week after week, month after month, the consummation of my thoughts desperately longs for the rains to fall.

My window of opportunity to bewail all within. Tears camouflaged by the torrents from above.

I cried in December.
I await this moment. when my tears, as chameleons flow lucidly clothed in disguise. The blessed rainfall that others bemoan, I seek out and stand behind as the curtain falls.

I cried in December
To the ovations of my heart... Born anew until the next venue...

CHAPTER II

THE "*COMMUNITY*"

By the age of 17 I immigrated to Israel as a returning minor.

Lived on a kibbutz for 2 years to learn Hebrew and work in the fields. Then enlisted into the army and by 20 I married into a religious cult unofficially called "*the nation*" or "*the community*". So... What is a community? Being part of a whole? Being part of a group of men and women leading a common life according to a rule? Looking back I have to ask myself...If I, (man and woman) was made in the image of God, am I not the representation of the whole? Why do I have to suffice with just a part? Am I not the whole? If I am whole, what was happening in my life, in my soul, in my thoughts and emotions that required me to allow myself to become fragmented? To allow my being to become divided?

The fragmented, divided me was given a new name...Elianah Baht Israel (baht Israel = daughter of Israel), and later on after marriage Elianah eshet A., (the wife of A.). When I discovered the "*community*", the cult, I was serving in the IDF, (Israeli Defense Forces), looking for a home away from home. A home away from my soul. Not realizing that my soul was home, the ultimate home. I felt so special!!! I wanted to feel a part of something! A part of this *"community"* according to the *"rule"*. And so started my journey through my own self imposed, self realized purgatory... a condition or place of temporary punishment, suffering, and atonement. In one sentence I would describe my life in the *"community"* **as a very religious experience in a penal colony.**

Their indoctrination of being holy and divine was intorduced to me via love. Love for god, love for your *"lord"*, love for the messia, (the "spiritual" leader) , love for the *"community"*. I was assailed with love bombing . They drugged me with love, admiration, validation, affection, adoration, flattery, laser beam attention, responsiveness and sexual and non-sexual touching. They hung on my every word and created a sense of instant rapport, connection and intimacy until I was hooked and reeled in. One never wants to be guilty of not loving god or not loving your *"lord"* who is in the image of god, or the messiah who is god on earth.

Being Israeli, Jewish and black was a huge thing, especially for the "*spiritual*" leader of the cult and his governing body of mostly men and a select few women. The red carpet was rolled out for me. Oh did I feel special! I was 19 years old with a new mission and purpose. I sank my teeth in, put my heart in my hands and tried to be the best member of this "*cult / community*" I could be. I became a doctor, a scholar, a wife, a mother, a "*saint*", and a zealot, and not necessarily in that order. I really believed this was the path that would save me. Being so young and naive I couldn't see the picture from the outside in. I only saw through the eyes of my emotions. Through eyes of wanting so much to be made pure and be forgiven for the sins of my past, of the sins of my childhood.

When I first met members of the cult, I was living on my base and very soon after meeting the "*saints*", I moved into a "*nation*" house. On weekends I traveled "*home*" to the cult, took off my uniform and changed into "*my culture*"... long dresses and turbans. I studied hard and incorporated these studies into my life. What to eat, what to wear, what to think. I was being prepared. My thoughts became divided, my emotions became divided, my choices became divided and after all of this division I was finally ready to give myself to the cause.

I systematically became brainwashed or mind controlled in order to change the way I thought, to subvert my free will and restrict my independent judgment . The aim was to undermine my own self reliance. Gradually coming to a place wherein I would trust the insights of the group leadership rather than trust in my own judgment. And all the while feeling holy and divine. All the while feeling special. All the while building a life for my future children and I founded upon a platform of fear. When people live in fear they will look outside of themselves for something, for anything to protect them from what they have been manipulated to fear. Fear is the greatest of all mass mind manipulation techniques. This physical world is the manifestation of either the fear or the love that is your consciousness.

The first event I participated in, while still in the IDF, was an evening of live band music and an after party. It was during the party that I met my future husband. We danced and talked all night until 6 AM. We were one of two couples left at the party along with the dj. As he turned to take me home, I literally heard my voice in my head saying, "*This is your husband*". After that it was a wrap. His father supported, encouraged and promoted our relationship in deed, spirit and words. Even though he (my future husbnd), was going to be engaged to his childhood sweetheart. We had an instantaneous connection, if only primal at first.

Being in love with him was problematic from the start. First of all he was involved with his childhood sweetheart. I was not a part of the "*community*", nor considered black. I was the Israeli Jew with an amazing sun tan. There were "*commuity*" events I wasn't allowed to participate in, in order to prevent me from being in close proximity to or distract him from his intended. Behind the scenes, however his father and the leader of the "*community*" were hard at work ensuring the continued connection between us on the down low. Unbeknownst to me they needed him to get Israeli citizenship through me. Eventually he became the liason, legal and otherwise between the "*community*" and the Israeli public He also rose through the ranks of leadership internally.

I became pregnant some time after he was engaged to his childhood sweetheart. Living under the same roof, in the same house together with his father the prince, doing everything possible to provide the mental, emotional and physical space for us to spend time together didn't lend itself to us staying away from one another. It became the scandal of the century. At least it played out like a major scandal. Their engagement was annulled. We had 30 days to get married. A decree went out from house to house with a scripture about "*flies sticking to shit*", or some other punitive, humiliating or degradating writing. Only family could participate in the ceremony and we were not allowed to wear white. I was ostracized by the "*saints*" for at least 5 years. I remember counting exactly 7 people, including the leader, my father in law, my 3 mothers in law and 2 other "*saints*" that spoke to me during these 5 years. Initially we lived in the house with my husband's family. Afterwards we moved to a home which already housed four other families... 30 children with two on the way and 10 adults.

I was so in love, so enamoured. I went for it hook, line and sinker. He was everything. The air that I breathed, the dreams that I dreamed, my every waking moment was about him. This was not just about my emotions. Outwardly it was also what was expected of me. To serve my "*lord*", (husband). It was expected of me to "*kneel so he may rise*" and you damn sure better love it! I accepted this as if my very life depended on it. Meals were on time, house was clean, eventually with the birth of our childen they were all in order, excelled in school, in the "*community*", and were an example of good behavior.

I was pregnant every year for 16 years. All of my children are between 1 and 2 years apart. Where there are 2 years between 2 children, I had a miscarriage. So yes every year for 16 years. I also nursed every year for 16 years. And I was left to deal with it all. He immediately after our wedding, found work in another city up north. He would be gone for 2 - 3 weeks at a time and come home for 24 hours.

For years I cried and cried about being alone all of the time, about never going anywhere or doing anything, about not spending time with my husband, of him not taking me anywhere. After 8 years he finally confessed to me... "*Just like I would never go to a hotel with 10 suitcases, and I would never eat food out of a container on a bus.... I don't want anyone asking me..... 'What? She's pregnant again'*? I was horrified! "*You're ashamed of me*", I replied. No he just didn't feel like having that conversation with people outside of the "*community*" because they wouldn't understand. "*So you're ashamed*". Before I knew it very tender and delicate words spewed forth from my mouth.... "*well it was your dick, ain't nobody else been up in there, so you must be ashamed of your dick*". And there it was... once again tainted with the "*mark of the beast*", the jealous wife,

Because everywhere he went, parties, events, his shows, always always there was some cute, young,unpregnant, fine "thang" going along for the ride and the adventure. So naturally it was all about me being jealous.

He also confessed he kept me pregnant on purpose so I would have to stay home with the children and he could move on and live his life. And I thought it was because we loved eachother... LMAO! Jokes on me. I can remember consciously thinking if I loved him enough for the both of us everything would work out fine. Everything did work out fine from the stand point of the "*community*". I did kneel, way down in the dirt, so he could rise, and rise he did. He became the liason, legal and otherwise between the "*community*" and the Israeli public and rose through the ranks of leadership internally.

He was an excellent provider, a good husband, and a good father in the beginning . However due to the intense pressure of the leadership and the "*saints*", this was very short lived. We were too connected. We had an ease about ourselves that was innate. This was disturbing to the "*powers that be*". If he was seen helping me with the family or chores around the house, he would hear, "*Don't you want a woman in your life that will treat you like a king*"? Or, "*If you had another wife you wouldn't have to do this... you could be a king*".

The gestapo like verbal and emotional pressure was so intense that we both caved in to it. He taking on the example of the ones that came before him... *if it doesn't work out with her and the children you can get another wife and kids and have another family*. This became his non verbal mantra, nothing and no one was going to get in his way. I caved in to the pressure by beating myself up for not being a better wife, for not being perfect according to their definition. I didn't know I had a choice to do or think otherwise. There must be evil in me if I have a problem with or am offended by the behavior of other "*sisters*" especially when it is focused on treating me like pure - d- unadulterated shit.

Once we stayed at a hotel for three days while he performed there. I waited up all night for him to return after his show, he finally returns at 6am. He spent the night with some one he met at the hotel. Then later invited her to our room to take a shower. The most painful part of these memories is coming to terms with how naive and stupid I was. At eight months pregnant my bedroom door was slammed in my face by one of his admirers. They wanted to continue their conversation.

Five course meals he enjoyed, sent to him by various girlfriends while the children and I looked on and tried to make ends meet. There were a couple of "*sisters*" I did like during their pursuit of him. However the minute he caught on that we were getting along he immediately lost interest and ulitmately blamed it on me. When we went to an event it was always with an entourage. He was either on security with the leader or his father. On the rare occasion we did go to a party together or an affair I was ignored most of the night while he mingled, flirted and danced.

One such party he was hot and heavy in pursuit of his now wife. Neither of them wanted me there. It was a major event, very cowded. They danced most of the time together and I sat on the side because he refused to dance with me. Finally I got up and danced with both of them, like other plural relationships in the "*community*". When the song ended another came on and both of them froze not wanting me there. I suggested we dance together again they both refused and she pushed me. I saw the hand coming to push me and I blocked it. I'm a funkin tree stump... I ain't goin nowhere! But she did. I blocked her and she went flying. It was dark so only a select few noticed what happened.

He hollared out to one of the priests there, who was on the dance floor no less, to send for security to get me and escort me out of the party. I was crazy and a danger to everyone. The priest hadn't seen what happened. He looked at me. I acted like I didn't know what was going on. So nothing came of it that night. You know the saying, "*It's always darkest before dawn*"? Well by dawn the next morning the black clouds of hell and damnation came down and I was informed I was on house arrest and being investigated by every entitiy of their government due to my unholy behavior and not fulling the definition of what a "*woman of yah*" is. Oh.... I forgot... I was also pregnant with what would have been our 12th child, my 16th pregnancy.

I had been spotting off and on for 3 weeks prior to the party. The morning after the party I was informed of the conditions of my punishment and investigation. I was also scheduled to go to the hospital to get a D&C. The baby had died but would not pass out of my sytsem. I was an emotional, physical wreck. All I wanted was a soft place to fall. To be held up when I just wanted to disappear. To be able to have a moment of weakness wherein I knew without a shadow of doubt he would be there.

The thinking was, if they could break me down and make me more subservient, they could use me politically, to promote their agenda with the Israeli public. All the while my husband was focused on proving his mahood. For one is not a real man unless he has more than one woman. While the wife proves herself loyal by self deprication, self hate and self denial of all things that are her birthright.

I allowed myself to be humiliated, degraded, oppressed and depressed in an effort to be seen as a "*daughter of yah*". To be accepted as a divine wife. I allowed myself to persist in an environment wherein he was god and the center of the universe. If everyone in the family needed a comb he would buy 2 combs. One for the children and I... and one for him. If he had some food he would eat it in front of me and never never offer me anything not even a bite. And so it was with EVERYTHING. I always thought there was something wrong with me because I was never happy, never fulfilled and always alone. I was nothing, insignificant, ... often I wanted to disappear. I wanted to disappear. I wanted to disapper. **BUT MY CHILDREN**!!!

The indoctrination, oppression and suppression of the female becomes more intense after marriage. It is all about what the woman has to do, what she has to think, and what she has to feel.

How she is responsible and accountable for everything and everyone else, in an effort to raise up her "*lord*", her husband. The man does not have to love the woman. Just marry her and figure out how to love her as time goes on. This becomes very problematic if time does not reveal or allow the emotion of being in-love to manifest. It becomes even more intense and problematic if other wives are involved. In fact the phrase falling in love was eradicated from their vocabulary. Romance was a Greco-Roman concept and therefore wicked

Then here comes "*divine marriage*" (polygyny)...**OH JOY!!!** A man can have seven wives based on the scripture Isaiah 4:1. The idea is for all of them to get along. The lifestyle dictates that the only thing required between the women is to say good morning, good night, what does "*our lord*" need. Even though "*being your brother or sister's keeper*" is preached, in actuality the way of life demands that the wife or wives totally embrace and exemplify the art of the "*long suffering servant*". Otherwise she will be forever stained with the "*Mark of the Beast*"... **she's jealous** and **she**

doesn't want him to have another wife*...* tattooed on her soul for everyone to see and for everyone to judge.

In all I have experienced, and witnessed in other women experiencing polygany, aka **"divine marriage"**, in this environment and in literally studying the doctrine of *"divine marriage"* as preached and taught by the leader and his consorts as a cornerstone of *"the preferred order of yah"*, I came to the conclusion that it was set up and institutionalized in the *"community"* with the purpose of being one of the means to destroy the feminine. Ultimately at some point the woman feels left out, slighted, humiliated, betrayed, degraded and neglected.

In my mind I could not understand how some one would go through the process of getting up, getting dressed, leaving her house, and walking or traveling to another *"sister's"* house in order to persecute her in her own home all in the name of *"divinity"* or *"divine marriage"*. As time went on I learned that the etymological, (word origin), definition of divine meant the worship of Zeus, who was a whore mongering incestuous god who married his sister, Hera through trickery and rape. AND THERE IT WAS...I was stained for life again with the **Mark of theBeast**...*"she's jealous"* and *"she doesn't want her lord to have another wife"*.

The main platform of the "*community*" is The *"**preferred order of yah**"* ... yah-man-woman-children. A linear system of being demoted to the lowest common denominator. The man pursues god, the woman pursues the man and the children pursue the parents. Whose preference was it? Who would choose to voluntarily be demoted or have others above them in estimation? I guess the women and the children would. I chose to be demoted not knowing what I was doing. All the while thinking it was holy and divine. The degradation and demotion continued. We taught it to our sons and instilled it in our daughters. Whenever the pain of it all came into question the concept of the *"long suffering servant"* was advocated, pursued and demanded.

Life in the cult was also based upon the "*greater laws*" (versus the "*lesser laws*"). The greater laws dictated what you **can't** do, (versus the lesser laws dictating what you can do). The greater laws reminding you of lack, how you are not enough, how you have to improve yourself, how you are not meeting the mark. A constant day in day out symphony of long suffering servitude enshrined in a state of lack and not meeting the mark. The shrine of this existence being the outward manifestation of the impoverished living conditions, the impaired state of the marriages, relationships, the devolution of the feminine and the confusion of the children.

This was my life. I cried almost everyday for 20 years. I was a sinner. Otherwise why would I feel so bad. If this was truly the "*Kingdom of God*" and this was truly the way to redemption, the only way I could feel so lost was if I was not on the right path. My everyday was filled with beating myself up because I wasn't good enough. I used to say I was the loneliest married woman in the world. However, somewhere in the midst of all of this misery

I was blessed to find some kind of solace. I discovered moments in every day that would harbor happiness affording me wrinkles in time to discover the inner strength to carry on and the desire to continue living. This solace, this happiness I found in my children.

In retrospect, I would have to say my father was the most powerful force in my agony!!! From a very young age, he daily informed me I was ugly, not human and didn't deserve to exist on this earth. Adding ingredients such as sexual violation, beatings, and the occult lends itself to agony, fear, terror, and "aloneness". Not loneliness... ALONENESS. Despite the fact that he wasn't physically present in my adult life he became cloned in every aspect of my life in the "*community*". He manifested in the leader of the cult... being influenced or participating in despotism, the occult / hidden agendas / secret society bullshit / affiliation. He manifested in my ex father in law... The father I always wanted, always needed, always looked for and in the end did a 180 degree about face and becme one of three banes of my existence... He manifested in my personal mentor and dean of the "*community*" college, a prince... his intellect, his genius, his scope of multi dimensional knowledge and teachings. The intellectual as well as spiritual connection he and I shared. He saw my worth, he validated me, and he protected me. He manifested in my husband. My father was the first man I learned how to love and taught me how to be loved. Being that I was taken out of cycle at such an early age, he was also the first man I learned to be in love with. The dynamics of this relationship was replicated in the dynamics between my husband, (*lord*) and I.

Once we handed over our marriage to the exploits of the cult and it's foundation of "**GROUP THINK**", this same exact sentiment was manifest in the attitude of disdain, never being good enough, and an endless cycle of re-inventing the wheel in an effort to keep me distracted, so as to lengthen, enlarge, and deepen the gulf of the connection between my soul, spirit, and emotions. He manifested in the day in and day out platform of "*your guilty until proven innocent*", encased in a system of crime and punishment wherein the only reward was to receive an imaginary title by an imaginary messiah and his imaginary god, which I activated and gave power to as me, myself and I, (my soul, my spirit and my emotions), became dimmer and dimmer.

Looking back I would have to say my husband had been looking for a way out all along. A way out of our lives – a way out of being responsible for 11 children and a wife. As I too was looking for a way out of the marriage, a way out of the "*community*". A way out of the seemingly endless onslought of everything and anything that I didn't like and didn't want in my life. It was my last pregnancy – it would have been our twelfth child. The fetus died in my womb and wouldn't pass. I went to the hospital to have a D&C. I was sick and feverish after carrying a dead fetus inside of me for three weeks. Upon arriving home from the hospital my husband had a show, (he's an entertainer, singer). I asked if he could call and check on me later on in the evening.

By then our marriage was finished. It had been for a long time but I was in denial. I couldn't face it. I was looking for anything to hold on to. To give me that last dose of energy to try again. To keep holding on. That phone call for me was the last hope. I gave up on everything else. I gave up on walking and talking, (never happened, never will). I had given up on being taken out, (never happened never will). I had given up on being treated special, on being remembered on my birthday... never happened never will....

That phone call meant everything to me. It would mean in spite of everything, he really did care, somehow someway. He really did want me in his life somehow someway. In a moment of weakness, 3 weeks prior, I leaned on his shoulder and asked, *"what am I going to do with another baby? What I am going to do with 12 children?"*, he replied, *"What would you do if I was dead or not here? Take your life into your own hands and deal with it"*?. This phone call meant he didn't mean what he said.

I waited for his call. The call he would make to check on me. The call would mean he in fact did love me. It never came. I couldn't sleep. I stayed up all night watching the phone, willing it to ring. Finally about 2:30 am he walked in the door. I spoke, asked how he was – how the show was. Then I asked why he didn't call to check on me. "*I just didn't feel like being bothered*". My heart stopped. My world ended – my light dimmed until it was completely gone. I noticed he was wearing a new garment/suit. One I didn't recognize. I asked where he had gotten the garment from. His girlfriend made it. As well as his Keepah and his crocheted shoes.

He was with her all night and took her to his performance. Even brought back the food I asked some one to cook for him. The girlfriend apparently also prepared food for him. I lost it. I grabbed him by the collar. I cried and pleaded, I begged. "*Why, why, why? Why couldn't you just call me? Why couldn't you check on me?*" Over and over again. His reply, "*Because I didn't feel like it*". The same reply over and over again. I continued to beg and plead. Please get some one to help us. "*I'm not doing shit*". Then get some one to help me. I can't do this anymore. "*I'm not doing shit*". All the while I tussled with him. I wouldn't let go of his collar. He hollered out to the children – to my oldest son – he was only 14. My husband, 100x stronger than me and 1000x faster, yet he was calling out to my oldest son, 15 years old at 3am to help him.

Finally we calmed down and went into the bedroom. I pleaded again and again for outside help, for some kind of counseling. "*I am not doing shit*" he replied time and again. I then grabbed his keepah, (skull cap), and scissors. Then proceeded to cut it up. I said I would continue to do crazy things until he got some one to come over and help. He still refused. He sent my oldest son to get a crowned brother, (a governmental official from the "community") – a neighbor. He happened to be on his way over to our house anyway ("*community*" business). My husband played dumb. I of course was the guilty party.

He wanted me banished from the house, from the city, from the region from the children and punished indefinitely. He said I was violent and I was a danger to the children. Their lives were in imminent danger. He stated that I threatened the children on other occasions with scissors. He accused my mother and I of coming together in order to do all kinds of terrible things against the "*community*". The crowned brother asked him what he wanted to do? He packed his bags and said he would be staying with his father – the Prince , the leader's childhood friend and right hand man. That was 11 years ago…. The night he left was the first night I slept peacefully in 14 years of being married.

At 6am I called one of the Israeli teachers from Akhvah school (the "community" school functioned under the auspices of the Ministry of Education in Israel). I decided to involve her in order to protect myself. I knew without a doubt the cult could not afford to have their one and only authentic Israeli born / Jewish descendent of a holocaust survivor **publicly** banished and separated from her also Israeli born Jewish children, from her very young children, (eleven children ages one year to fifteen years old). I told her what happened, what my husband was accusing me of and how he wanted to banish and punish me indefinitely.

We put our heads together and came up with a plan. I kept all of children home from school, with the exception of my oldest son and one of the older girls. He needed his space and time to think. The teacher called another Israeli teacher from Akhvah school and explained the situation to her. Together they approached the vice principal of the school who was one of the leaders in the cult. They showed great concern about the absence of all of my children from school that day. They insinuated they had heard rumors about family problems and requested that he, the vice principal, investigate what happened. At the same time they made subtle threats... no matter what the situation was, the children needed to be with their mother and the *"community"* better not separate the mother from her children. Whether this worked or not I will never know. However, I was never banished to Tiberius.

The same morning I woke all of the children as if they were going to school. I brought them together in my room. I apologized for what happened. We stood in a circle, held hands and prayed. I asked that we pray for their father. To pray that Yah watch over him, that he stay strong, that Yah continue to bless him. I felt I had to do this in order to keep their father in a positive light. I thought I was being strong for them – being godly by being selfless in their sight. By praying for their father and for them – for the family. Afterwords I spoke with my oldest son alone. I talked and talked, and talked. Always shining the light on his father, always praising him and raising him up. Neutralizing the situation, neutralizing him. The praying together before hand helped. Finally I saw the light return to his eyes again and I knew that somehow, someway, someday he would be alright.

Sure enough later that morning the vice principal called inquiring as to the whereabouts of the children and asking if there was a problem. I told him what happened. During that first week of separation, whenever my husband and I spoke, it always ended up in an argument. I continued to beg and plead for him to help mend our marriage. To make it work,. My words fell upon deaf ears. He was too involved in pursuing his manhood via of his relationship with his girlfriend to care.

It was Yom L'Mokerim season, (like Christmas but with another name). I couldn't go. I was inactive, (set aside for two weeks because of the miscarriage, unclean). This was my husband's chance to go out on the town and be amongst the saints with his girlfriend. He could finally impress upon his father and the other leaders that he was a *real* man. Of course he was, he had another woman. I however was at home, (inactive... bleeding) with eleven children under 15 and no help.

According to the laws of inactivity I wasn't allowed to do any housework or function in the kitchen. Besides which, physically I wasn't able to. I asked my husband's permission to receive help from another sister or two. He said *"**absolutely not**"*! My children helped. They always did. Even my ten year old son pulled a couple of cook days. In addition to this, all of the children had Yom L'Mokerim parties. They all needed new clothing – which I had to sew. Somehow, someway we made it through. While my husband pursued his other life.

After the first week week of separation he told me he had been officially informed that he was not allowed to come to the house. Most of our meals for the first two months were cream of wheat – breakfast, snack and dinner. The children ate lunch at the *"community"* cafeteria after school. Before my husband moved out he purchased a sack of organic wheat berries intending to grow wheat grass for wheat grass juice. This is what we ate for two months. I ground the wheat berries, rinsed them and cooked them – voila – cream of wheat. About four weeks into this dietary program one of my daughters told her father what we were eating. That we had no other food. Just wheat berries. *"Halleluyah, I don't have to buy groceries, keep grinding"* was his reply. All the while they watched him eat his five course meals – ice cream shakes – dates, snadwiches, casseroles, etc., catered to him by his family, his girlfriend or anyone else wanting t get his attention.

On several occasions when the children visited their father, they would ask for some of his food and were regularly told, *"no this food is for your father"*. After the initial two months we also ate a lot of oatmeal and other grains. We rarely had fruit. My husband eventually bought groceries once every six to eight weeks.

After having written this last portion I went into the bathroom and cried. I have held it in for so long. Trying to be strong. Wanting to be strong, having to be strong. Not wanting to be weak. I wasn't just heart broken as a result of the things that transpired between us. I was totally devastated. By the time everything was finally over I didn't have a heart, or lungs or any other vital organs. I was dead and had been dying for quite some time. In picking up the pieces of my life I had to figure out how to acquire or create a new heart, new lungs new vital organs, to rebuild them, recreate them. To create a new world, a new reality, new DNA wherein not only did he not exist but he never did. I had to be reborn again as if I had no prior knowledge of anything that was even remotely related to him, my marriage or the cult.

At age 36, I officially became a single mom of 11 children. My oldest was 15 and the youngest was 1 year old... going from house to house begging for food for the family... growing vegetables in order to feed them.... getting chastised by "*community*" leaders for using water to grow the food. Being chastised for getting the house painted, buying new furniture and appliances because I did not have approval from my "*lord*" (my husband). Even though he was neither present nor involved in any way. They wanted the money I spent on upgrading the children's lives from living in a dungeon to living in a home.

Not having hot water winter after winter... heating water on the stove in order to bathe everyone... Washing everyone's cloths by hand because we didn't have a washing machine... Sewing all of our clothing... no money to buy clothes... Leadership of the cult trying to literally kill me mentally physically spiritually... Being followed, even coming into my home and looking through my things in my absence. Having my children spying on me unbeknownst to them they were actually spying.

When the furniture and the appliances arrived and it was being assembled, the children started jumping up and down and laughing. Watching every move touching everything. This was one of those wrinkles in time. One of those moments where I found happiness. Seeing, sharing, and experiencing my children's happiness was monumental! It was what kept me gasping for air. It was what compelled me to daily choose life while literally looking death in the eye. During these moments I could even be heard saying out loud, "*I want to live*"! This was my cycle. Verbally and consciously affirming I want to live so my children may live!!!

I felt as if each day during different times of the day the question of LIFE or DEATH stood before me looking for an answer like a troll sitting under a bridge allowing one to cross if his question is answered correctly. The troll being me getting in the way of the real me. The me that was screaming and clawing to come alive in totality instead of glimpses of what I knew I could be or was supposed to be. I chose literally, consciously and intentionally, mentally, emotionally, spiritually and physically, LIFE... every time **for the sake of my children.**

Choosing the domino of life because of my children progressively opened the gateway to receiving and conceiving other reasons to live. I don't want my children to struggle anymore than they already have... I'll be goddamned if I give up before I, me, myself and I, have had a chance to manifest my personal dreams, desires, goals and wishes... because I really do believe in life!!! JUST BECAUSE LIFE AT SOME POINT HAS

TO BE CONSISTENTLY AWESOME!!! And I want to know what that feels like. I want to see my family, immediate and kin folk get together again the way we, the children and I, dream about! And after all is said and done I WANT MY LIFE BACK!!!!!!!!!!!!!!!!!! Last but not least, who the fuck wants to die tired, miserable, lonely and unaccomplished?

fter he moved out my husband and I were called to official meetings. Present at the meeting was a representative from every level of leadership within the "*community*". The committee put in charge of my "*marital*" situation was supposed to be evaluating everything. Each meeting began with all of the committee members including my husband holding hands and praying. Everyone was a governmental official except me. Only afterward was I invited into the room. The minister read a letter in which it was stated that we've been having problems for a long time, the problems continued to get worse and they didn't know what the solution was. Therefore we were to be separated indefinitely. No communication was allowed between us. The minister was to be the liaison between us as concerns financial issues and my husband was to be escorted to the house by security in order to remove all of his belonging.

The meeting ended. I pretended to be sad, I even had tears in my eyes. It was Motsai Shabbat, (Saturday Night), March 2, 2001, our 14th wedding anniversary. The day we were officially married and the day we were officially separated. I saw this as divine intervention. I left the meeting looking sad and despondent. I closed the door, everyone else had stayed behind, I don't know what they were discussing, but I literally skipped all of the way home, with a big smile on my face, chanting, *"free at last, free at last, thank god I'm free at last"*!

My husband never came to the house to remove his belongings and neither did security. They really didn't have to. That same night I packed up all of his belongings. The suitcase was waiting outside of my room. After two weeks I asked permission to send the suitcase to his father's house. Afterwords I proceeded to remove every single item that reminded me of him, of our marriage and of the cult. I threw away a lot of my clothing, pictures, sheets, decorations etc. You name it, I threw it away if it had any sort of attachment to the last fourteen years. For me it was over, it never was... it never even happened. It took me about a year to throw away our wedding pictures. I wanted to do this with a clean heart. Not out of anger or bitterness or revenge. Initially I sent the pictures to my husband, he sent them back to me. I threw them away.

Each meeting was a nightmare. I was asked questions and expected to respond with the answers they wanted to hear. When I didn't, I was systematically tarred and feathered, burned at the stake, and crucified. Each meeting ended with the prince hollaring and demanding I leave the room. Commanding me to return a week later after changing everything I had so far stated. Each meeting ended with me being told I was doomed to die like the children of Israel died in the wilderness, I was evil and wicked. I was destroying my children. Only after I left the room did they once again hold hands and pray.

Unbeknownst to them, this was the best thing that could have ever happened to me! This was the perfect motivation and inspiration to want something, anything that would bring more joy and happiness to my life and the lives of my children. We were taught that the "Kingdom of Yah" is a new civilization. A civilization of men governing men that are governed by Yah. The word civilization is synonymous with slavery. It is dependent on giving up the freedom of personal choice in order that the group organization, (or group thought), might have preference, (remember, the "*preferred order of yah*"). Beyond the family no organization is necessary. Personal responsibility is the pathway of freedom.

Besides these committee meetings, the next six months were basically the same. A day to day challenge in feeding and taking care of the children... no furniture, no beds, no closets, no fridge.

The cupboards stayed bare. Daily and weekly I would go to various homes and ask for vegetables so I could prepare a meal. My children would often do the same. It was so degrading, so humiliating. One day a friend of mine, a brother, gave me some plantlings... broccoli, cauliflower, onions, cabbage, lettuce and celery.

He was a farmer and really wanted to help us but he too was in financial straits. However he did have these plants. He taught me how to grow and take care of them. When the harvest was ready we had broccoli soup, broccoli casserole, broccoli salad and so on. It turned out to be a really amazing project for the children and I! A hard and seemingly unjust situation turned into a wonderful experience the children and I were blessed to share with one another. We watered the garden everyday, we watched the vegetables grow and harvested what we were going to eat. In the midst of it all somehow someway we continued to be blessed. My children and I became closer and as time went on we enjoyed each other more and more.

The night my husband packed his shit and moved out was the impetus that motivated me to unconsciously open myself up to the concept that there may be another way. At this point I was not determined to create a way out. It was the just realization that I didn't have to live like this anymore! IT WAS THE REALIZATION THAT I HAD A CHOICE. I came to believe one must suffer only in order to finally come to the conclusion that one does not ever have to suffer ever in life! Not physically, not financially, not emotionally, not spiritually, not in any way shape or form! Allowing myself to suffer, whether consciously or unconsciously, started a chain reaction allowing others the right to make me suffer and the right to help me suffer. In so doing I am handing over my conscious right to self-destiny and self-control. This same chain reaction continues onto my children who by way of example will grow up and repeat history. Is this then the legacy I would choose to leave them…suffering and misery?

I want my children to know they have a choice. They can choose life…they can choose to be truly free…they can choose their destiny and then govern that destiny. They can choose joy and happiness. I saw the anger, the pain, the bitterness and the frustration they held within even as young as they were. All of the misery and suffering I experienced will have been worth it if they could learn in their very early years what took me 41 years to figure out. Then in turn each one of them can show some one else what they have learned thereby starting a chain reaction of their own, a pro-life, pro-creation, pro-happiness chain reaction.

The morning after he moved out I woke possessing a sense of relief. This conscious physical realization endowed me with the knowledge that I had a choice. I could choose not to suffer. I could choose happiness, my OWN happiness, and define for myself what makes me happy without feeling wicked or evil for being qualified to do exactly that. A sense of quiet settled over my being for the first time since childhood when my escape was nature, the sunsets, the rain, the grass and the trees. Sitting for hours watching the rain, smelling it, feeling the wind, enjoying the sound. At some point I would become the rain, the sunset, the birds, the crickets. I immerged myself with the elements, the fauna and the flora, thereby eluding the scourge of the topography of my life while incurring boundless, timeless moments of peace. There is no death in these moments, no pain, no suffering, no darkness. Only life, only timelessness, only eternity.

I am reminded of a conversation I had with an older brother from the "*community*" years ago. I was working in a hotel at the Salt Sea, (Dead Sea), as a chamber maid. I happened to see this brother one day and he asked me what I had been doing. I told him about working in a hotel. He was furious. He started yelling, "*What are you doing?! You're an Israeli, you can do anything here. Why are you wasting your time? What are you going to leave your children while working in a hotel as a chambermaid? What are you going to leave your children*"?

I thought about this question over and over again for days. He was right, what would I leave my children? What inheritance, what legacy would be manifested in their lives? I thought and meditated. Then it came to me. What is the most precious gift I could give or leave for my children? I decided to leave them the earth. To give them the universe and all that is beyond and within. I would give them the keys to happiness and joy. As I learn, they will learn. In learning to manifest consciously with my emotional guidance system as the screen through which I determine what I want and what I look forward to, I will pass it on to them.

THE ONLY FERTILE GROUND FOR FREEDOM OR CAPTIVITY IS YOUR SOUL!!!

I think about me and who I am. I can feel me, the extended version of me, the other 90% me that is not physical. It almost feels like the real me has to fit through a bottle neck in order to experience the physical me. So I have to squeeze tight in order to become one with the physical me. One would think this bottle neck only squeezes forth the best, the most positive and the sweetest parts but instead, along with the best of me being squeezed through, also came the conditions wherein insecurity, self doubt and fear would flourish as if my life was/is a Petri dish. Am I the scientist then, experimenting unconsciously with this illusion that is called my life?

Anyway.... I just want to be me, be safe, be happy, be successful, be prosperous and be free. I guess this is really what I am looking for!!! THE FREEDOM TO BE ME, DO ME, AND APPLY ME TO ANY GIVEN CIRCUMSTANCE WITH THE ULTIMATE GOAL OF BEING JOYFUL and in so doing open the door, hold the door open or point to the door wherein others may find personal salvation according to the dictates of their quest for freedom and fascination/joy/ happiness with themselves first and foremost and life.

JUST WANNABE ME AND BE FASCINATED WITH ME / LIFE!!!!! Whatever it was I worked hard to break through and overcome this type of behavior. It was similar to digging out a deeply imbedded disease or growth that became so comfortable within the environment it had invaded it almost seemed like a normal part of the host body.

Very early on I was able to move out of the village thereby affording me the opportunity to raise my children with less interference from the "community". My husband was always gone. I never could bring myself to call him *"lord"*, which became a bone of contention with the leadership, especially the crowned sisters, (the highest level of female leadership). He would come home every two to three weeks for twenty four to fourty eight hours and leave again. He worked in another city and lived there. After being away for eight years, he moved back home into the arms of the "spiritual" leader of the cult. The children and I were on the lower rungs of the preferred order of yah.

BREAKDOWN OF THE FAMILY SYSTEM

Placing the *"spiritual"* leader of the cult first (god-man-woman-child), or anyone else for that matter, started the breakdown of my family. Like a dog chasing its tail. The man pursues the leader, the woman pursues the man, and the children pursue the parents. The system wasn't structured for individual growth. A great source of one's power is the ability to connect with people, not controlling people. **I am that I am** is the highest statement a person / living soul can use in this world. It expresses the "bond" between the human self, the anointed higher consciousness self, and a knowing of one's true identity, one's destiny and the passage to higher dimensions.

I was taught diversity and tolerance by my mother. I was raised to treat people justly and never to look at a person's skin color, religion or gender. Taking on the image and personality of intolerance and prejudice was the opposite extreme of my upbringing… the opposite extreme of who I really was and who I was supposed to be. Why did I give all of this up so easily and willingly to some one or something that did not have my best interest at heart, or anyone else's for that matter? How did I allow myself to be in such denial about what was going on right in front of my eyes?

I chose some one else's *"preferred order"*. I chose some one else's concept of life and living because I allowed myself to be tricked into looking outside of myself for redemption and saving. I made a covenant with some one else instead of developing a covenant with my higher self...."*I AM THAT I AM*"... an even more literal translation would be... "*I WILL BE THAT WHICH I WILL BE*". The basis of my life should have been freedom and my purpose should have been joy. I was born free to discover different ways for manifesting and enhancing joy in my life. Instead I chose bondage, pain, and long suffering.

Through all of this I learned how to go within, dig deep and find a way to continue in spite of the external circumstances surrounding me at any given moment in time. It showed me where to go and reach in order to be strong and continue on. It showed me how to learn from every situation. I recently asked myself why I always choose the hard road. Maybe this is not for me to ask. Just do and learn and somewhere sometime I will be able to look back and understand the purpose behind the life choices I have made.

LEAVING THE "COMMUNITY"

After 20 years of living under a reign of fear and tyrannical control at the hands of the leader and his governing officials, my children and I escaped. This escape more so refers to a mental, emotional and spiritual self imposed captivity. I went through years of being humiliated, punished, used for political reasons (I was the only Israeli / Jew in the cult), and threatened with physical harm. When the governing body of the cult realized they couldn't get to me they proceeded to systematically and methodologically pursue my younger children in an effort to hurt or punish me and make me comply.

Soon after leaving, I began to see a change in the children. Either they were actually becoming more understanding or maybe they were just calming down. One of my goals was to get to a point wherein they were not so hostile to one another, wherein they would be able to communicate without being so offensive. Is this a learned trait left over from the years that we spent in "*the community*"? "*Shut up! Sit Down! You're on Ohnish (punishment)! You're a fool! You are wicked and evil*". Or was it just the baser part of me that connected with the baser part of a collective which had influenced the children to behave in such a manner.

Whatever it was I worked hard to break through and overcome this type of behavior. It was similar to digging out a deeply imbedded disease or growth that became so comfortable within the environment it had invaded it almost seemed like a normal part of the host body. Prayer helps, so does being positive. Staying positive is the only thing that keeps me from giving up. The task at hand sometimes seems so impossible. But I have no choice. This has to be done… "*One small step for Ilyana and her*

11 children, one big step for mankind".

My husband was the love of my life. He was everything to me. But now, when I see him I don't recognize him. I don't know him and don't feel as if I ever did. It is amazing what the mind can do in an effort to heal and survive. In so doing I have also been blessed to become a new and improved me... Some one that I have always wanted to be and didn't know how. Some one that I like and respect. Some one that likes and respects me and all of the layers of me. I no longer feel as if I have to hide any part of me from myself. I am learning how to be first on my list instead of last on everyone else's list. Maybe this then is the reason that I chose to go through this, that I chose this path. If so then I really should be thankful for all I experienced over these last 20 years within my marriage and within the cult. Then thankful I am!

I once heard a story about two angels that were traveling from place to place. They came upon a village and needed a place to stay. They arrived at the home of a very poor elderly couple that owned a cow which provided them with milk and was their only source of income. Even though the couple had nothing they gave the two angels all that they had to eat and gave them their bed to sleep in while they slept in the barn. The next morning when everyone awakened it was found out that the cow died during the night. The younger and less experienced of the two angels asked the other angel, *"how could you let this happen? You are an angel. This was their only sustenance and their only means of an income. How could you let this happen"*? The other angel replied, *"Nothing is as it seems."*

The angels continued on their way and once again needed a place to stay for the night. They arrived at the home of another couple that were very wealthy but very stingy. They offered them no food and allowed them to sleep in the basement even though they had ample rooms in the house to accommodate them. In the middle of the night the younger angel woke up and saw the older angel patching up a hole in the wall with plaster. This really confused him. He went back to sleep. In the morning he approached the older angel and expressed to him his confusion,

"I just don't understand. The first night you allowed the cow, the poor elderly couple's only source of nourishment and income to die, and last night you fixed the wall of the wealthy couple who were so stingy they wouldn't even feed us let alone let us sleep in one of their bedrooms in the house". The older angel replied, *"Nothing is as it seems".* The younger angel was still distraught. *"I just don't understand. You help the people that treated us badly and you allowed something terrible to happen to the people that gave us everything when they had nothing".* Once again the older angel replied, *"Nothing is as it seems. When we stayed with the poor elderly couple the death angel came to take the wife and I asked that he take the cow instead. When we stayed with the wealthy couple I noticed a hole in the wall and upon closer inspection saw that in the hole was a pot of gold. I fixed the wall because the wealthy couple did not deserve such a treasure. Nothing is as it seems".*

This story has carried me through many a hard day, many a hard times, and has helped me through many a difficult cross roads. During these times I continued to remind myself and even chanted over and over again out loud…"*Nothing is as it seems*"…*Nothing is as it seems*"…*Nothing is as it seems*". Time and time again this has been the case. Things look one way initially but given time the end result or the ultimate purpose is revealed. How would I have known twenty one years ago that a ten minute event would place me on a path of much turmoil, suffering and hardship? At least at the time it seemed and felt like turmoil, suffering and hardship. But it made me who I am today. Hopefully not all events or situations will endure this long. Some may last ten minutes and at times may seem like the last ten minutes of your life…"*Nothing is as it seems* "…"*Nothing is as it seems*".

My children and I became closer and as time went on we enjoyed each other more and more. Day after day I prayed…,"*Yah, if this is meant to be fixed please fix it. If it is meant to end please end it because I don't how to do it".* I also prayed daily that a man of yah would come into our lives. A guardian angel arrived in our midst, Dode. A musician, single, from Bermuda. In the beginning the children didn't like him. This didn't last long. He became our Dode, (uncle), our friend, our guide and our teacher. My personal soul friend and savior. He was Yah in our midst. He helped hold us together. He changed diapers, helped potty train, gave the children ample attention and helped me make it through everyday.

During the first year he moved in with us he talked to me all day every day about Yah. The Yah in me, the Yah in the children and in our lives. So many times I cried on his shoulder. My husband was gone all of the time so it was always Dode and I at home with the children. We became a family, so when my husband moved out we remained a family. Dode never took advantage of me or my girls. He always kept it "holy". He never crossed any lines. We spent many hours together as a family. Laughing, eating, talking. He continued to guide and strengthen the children and I. He never missed a beat. I learned so much from him. He helped to unlock the different doors to my spirit and my soul. Doors I didn't even know existed. We were so close that sometimes if we would see each other in public he would say, *"Baby girl you can't look at me like that. The "saints" will read it the wrong way"*. And sure enough they did. A few months after my husband moved out it was rumored that Dode was screwing the hell out of me. We both just laughed.

I had the opportunity to visit him in Bermuda. I asked him why he never crossed the line with me. He said that for the entire 3 years he lived with us he had lived in fear. He was never so afraid in his life. He didn't know if he would be able to stay strong. But he knew he had to. He said the children had been through enough pain and suffering already and they would be devastated if something like that would get out. Besides, I made him promise to be stronger than me. He kept his promise – even at times when I wish he wouldn't have.

As time went on I wrote letter after letter to the "**committee**" to no avail... the committee of representatives that were supposed to be dealing with my marital situation. All the while I thought my requests for food, clothing shoes etc. were being forwarded to the "*spiritual*" leader, they were in fact being forwarded to my husband. Nothing was ever done. Once I wrote a requisition to the "Ministry of Divine Distribution" asking for funds for clothing – shoes – furniture – food. I was told point blank that I was not able to receive any requisition monies. We went without heat for 2 winters, no hot water for one. Every time we wanted to bathe I would have to boil water on the stove.

One season we went 4 months without a washing Machine. Most of the wash I did by hand, once or twice a week I would send the larger pieces, such as sheets and towels to the homes of other members of the cult that lived in the neighborhood. One day my sister in law approached the crowned brother that functioned on the "*committee*" and asked him come to our house and see for himself how we were living. He came and walked through the entire house. He finally said to me, "*Elianah, I have to ask you, who's spirit is this, yours or your husband's? In all of my days in the "Kingdom" I have not seen anything like this*". As I mentioned earlier, no food, no fridge to put the food in, the cupboards were bare, no furniture, I had to sell some of it in order to support the children. No closets, we used old book shelves for the clothing.

I am still trying to understand who I am, where I come from and what lead me to this day – to this life and where I am going. Who am I really after the cult? What lead me to the cult and what was I really looking for? Thus I continue to write. It is like a cleansing. As I peal away the layers more is revealed and more becomes clear.

My main goal is to be happy and joyful and to prosper in this happiness and joy.. I continue to ask for guidance, strength, patience and knowledge in helping the children to heal.

Sometimes it is very frustrating for them. They want to see immediate results. They want to see immediate repercussions even amongst themselves. They have been so used to one method – and now emah, (mom), is using another method. The older children seem to understand as long as I continue to explain to them exactly what I am doing and what it is that I hope to accomplish. Life goes on and is good. I look forward to the rest of my life with my children, and finally being and becoming llyana.

ARISE

Lay down your weapon, oh ye son of war, Lost in your vision of grandeur, Captive in your dream of glory.

Praising the thunder of perdition, Sacrificing the alms of innocence.

Prepare the way for the souls you've become indebted to, hail the banner of destruction felled at your feet,

Bewail the cause of iniquity trapped in a wrinkle in time.

Finite, limited, veiled in deception of the powers that define your past, your present, your future.

Lay down your pride, oh ye son of war, awake upon the foundation of cosmic consciousness, ever entranced by your denial of change,

Ever transformed by your evolutionary upheaval. Paving the path of ascension, patrolling the karma of your existence.

Lay down your soul, oh ye son of war, captured by enemies from within, held hostage upon the altar of your metamorphosis.

Giving heed to the eternal flame, holding fast to wheels within wheels of infinite spirit, of infinite life.

Stand up, oh ye son of ma. Reap the harvests of your resurrection, display the aura of the inner light.

Arise to your purpose. Arise, Arise, to your life born anew.

CHAPTER III

LIFE AFTER THE "*COMMUNITY*"..... Letting go

I HAVE OFTEN FELT LIKE I'VE LOST SO MUCH TIME, SO MANY WEEKS, MONTHS AND YEARS, IN PURSUING THE PATHS WHEREIN THE DYE HAD BEEN CAST ON MY PERSONAL LIFE JOURNEY. I SAW THE NEED TO NOT ONLY REGROUP AND RE-EVALUATE, BUT TO BACK TRACK WHERE I COULD, IN ORDER TO ESTABLISH NEW PATHS AND NEW MEMORIES AS I REASSEMBLED THE PIECES OF

MY LIFE.

THIS BEING SAID, IT HITS ME THAT I HAVE SPENT MY ENTIRE ADULT LIFE RAISING MY 11 CHILDREN. THE LAST 10 YEARS I HAVE BEEN TRYING TO SAVE MYSELF AND MY CHILDREN FROM THE VERY SAME PATH I SET UP FOR US. IT WAS SET UP FOR ALL THE RIGHT REASONS... HAPPINESS, RIGHTEOUSNESS, FULFILLMENT, HEALTH, LONGEVITY, SECURITY, JUST TO NAME A FEW. BUT WHERE AND WHEN DID THE SWITCH COME?

THE SWITCH FROM EXCITEMENT, HOPE, AND ANXIOUSLY WAITING FOR DREAMS TO BE FULFILLED, TO MISERY, HOPELESSNESS, FEELING DOOMED, GUILT, AND LAST BUT NOT LEAST ANGER. THIS CHANGE OR TANSFORMATION OCCURRED WITHOUT ANY MAJOR PHYSICAL, GEOGRAPHICAL, OR OTHER TANGIBLE CHANGES TO THE LIFE I WAS LIVING, THE LIFE I SET UP FOR MY CHILDREN AND I.

HOW DID ALL OF THIS GO FROM ONE EXTREME TO ANOTHER. FROM HOPE TO DESPAIR, FROM EXCITEMENT TO DOOM, FROM FEELING SAFE AND SECURE, TO BEING PARANOID ABOUT WHO WAS WATCHING, AND WHAT THEY THOUGHT OF ME. HOW DO I GET AWAY NOT JUST FROM THE PHYSICAL CIRCUMSTANCES OF MY LIFE, BUT ALSO THE MENTAL, EMOTIONAL, PHYSICAL, AND SPIRITUAL PERSON I HAD BECOME, THAT I CHANGED INTO. IT IS SAID THE GOOD THING ABOUT ROCK BOTTOM IS THE ONLY WAY OUT IS UP. BUT ON THIS JOURNEY I FOUND THAT THE ONLY WAY TO GET OUT OF MY ROCK BOTTOM, WAS NOT UP BUT "IN".

WHEN CLIMBING UP ONE CAN AT SOME POINT SEE PROGRESS. "OK, I AM GOING UP, THE BOTTOM LOOKS FARTHER AND FARTHER AWAY, SO I KNOW I AM MAKING PROGRESS". WHEN I WENT INWARD INSTEAD OF UP, FOR YEARS I FELT BLINDED TO THE PROGRESS THAT WAS

BEING MADE, PERSONALLY, INDIVIDUALLY, AND AS A UNIT, AS A FAMILY.

GOING IN(WARD), WAS LIKE GOING THROUGH A NEVER ENDING WORMHOLE, WHICH MOST OF THE TIME LOOKED THE SAME AND FELT THE SAME. SO MANY TIMES I WANTED TO THROW MY HANDS UP, AND SAY, "THAT'S IT, FUCK THIS SHIT, I CAN'T DO IT ANYMORE, I AM READY TO GIVE UP THE GHOST, AND BE DONE WITH IT"! BUT MY CHILDREN..... IT IS THIS VERY THOUGHT...."BUT MY CHILDREN" THAT FOREVER KEEPS ME MOVING ONWARD, UPWARD AND INWARD IN MY QUEST TO FIND (inner) HAPPINESS, (inner) RIGHTEOUSNESS, (inner) FULFILLMENT, (inner) HEALTH, (inner) LONGEVITY, AND (inner) SECURITY.

I REALIZED THIS TRANSFORMATION BEGAN IN THE VERY SAME MOMENT I GAVE SOME ONE OR SOMETHING OUTSIDE OF MYSELF THE POWER TO DEFINE WHAT HAS

TO MAKE ME HAPPY, HOW I <u>HAVE</u> TO EXPRESS MY RIGHTEOUSNESS, HOW I HAVE TO LIVE, WHAT I HAVE TO WEAR, AND HOW I HAVE TO RAISE MY CHILDREN IN ORDER FOR ME / US TO MAKE IT THROUGH THOSE "PEARLY GATES". THE BEGINNING OF THE END OCCURRED WHEN I GAVE THIS POWER AWAY.

IN REGROUPING, REJEUVENATING, AND BEING REBORN AS ME, THE REAL ME, I HAD TO EMPOWER MYSELF WITH WHAT WAS INATELY MINE IN THE FIRST PLACE. "THE POWER TO DEFINE" WHAT WAS / IS BEST FOR ME. IN ORDER TO COME FULL CIRCLE I THEN TAUGHT THIS TO MY CHILDREN SO THEY IN TURN WOULD BE EMPOWERED.

ONE OF MY SONS SAID TO ME ONE DAY, "MOM I LISTEN TO YOU AND I LISTEN TO DAD, HOW DO I KNOW WHO IS RIGHT AND WHO IS WRONG, BECAUSE YOU BOTH MAKE SENSE"? I REPLIED, "IT ISN'T ABOUT WHO IS RIGHT AND

WRONG, IT IS ABOUT HOW "YOU" FEEL. IT IS ALL ABOUT YOUR HAPPINESS AND YOUR BLISS. YOUR EMOTIONS ARE THE BAROMETER... THE GUIDE POST TO LET YOU KNOW WHAT IS RIGHT FOR YOU. IF IT MAKES YOU FEEL GOOD TO FAST ON THE SABBATH THEN DO SO BECAUSE IT IS WHAT IS BEST FOR YOU, IT IS WHAT MAKES YOU FEEL GOOD AND WHOLE. BUT IF YOU FAST ON THE SABBATH BECAUSE SOME ONE TOLD YOU THAT YOU HAVE TO OR YOU WILL DIE... THIS IS ANOTHER ENERGY ALL TOGETHER.

YOU CAN LEARN SOMETHING FROM EVERY INDIVIDUAL WHOSE PATH CROSSES WITH YOURS. ARE THEY RIGHT OR WRONG IN THEIR THINKING, IN THEIR CULTURE, IN THEIR LIFESTYLE? I DON'T KNOW. BUT DO YOU EXPERIENCE AND ENJOY INNER PEACE, HAPPINESS, AND SATISFACTION AS A RESULT OF WHAT YOU DO, WHAT YOU THINK, AND WHAT YOU FEEL IN LIEU OF WHAT YOU LEARNED AND EXPERIENCED FROM ANY GIVEN

PERSON"?

I READ SOMEWHERE THAT WE CHOOSE OUR PARENTS BEFORE WE GET HERE, WE CHOOSE THE LIFE TEST WE ARE TO EXPERIENCE ON EARTH IN ORDER TO LEARN THE LESSON THEREIN. THIS LIFE LESSON MIGHT JUST BE CONTAINED IN THE 90% OF ME THAT HASN'T BEEN FULLY ACTIVATED. WE DO ONLY USE 10% OF OUR BRAINS... OF OUR CONSCIOUSNESS RIGHT? THEN IT STANDS TO REASON I HAVE SOME SAY SO IN WHAT I WOULD EXPERIENCE HERE BY TAPPING INTO THIS 90%.

IF THE PAST DOESN'T EXIST ANYMORE, AND THE FUTURE HASN'T HAPPENED YET, THE HERE AND NOW WOULD LOGICALLY BE THE MOST IMPORTANT MOMENT. WHAT IS HAPPENING NOW, WHAT I AM FEELING AND THINKING NOW IS THE DOORWAY TO THIS PART OF MY SUBCONSCIOUSNESS. BEING THAT THE NOW IS THE MOST IMPORTANT MOMENT THEN WHAT HAPPENED IN

THE PAST DOESN'T MATTER. HOW I GOT HERE DOESN'T MATTER. WHAT MATTERS TO ME IS DID I LEARN THE LESSON? WHAT WAS THE LESSON? DID I GET THE MESSAGE?

THE MESSAGE....I MATTER! THE LESSON....TO LEARN TO LOVE ME, ALL OF ME! DID I LEARN THE LESSON...YES! LOVING ME JUST FEELS SO MUCH BETTER THAN NOT LOVING ME! DID I GET THE MESSAGE? DO I MATTER? ABSOLUTELY 100% YES!!! WHY? BECAUSE IN ORDER TO LOVE ME I HAVE TO MATTER! WHEN I LOVE ME AND I MATTER, I INSTANTANEOUSLY FEEL JOY, BLISS, HAPPINESS, FULFILLED, AND SATISFIED, (IMMEDIATE GRATIFICATION IS SO MY THING)!!! IN LEARNING TO LOVE ME I FEEL MORE AND MORE CONNECTED TO EVERYTHING AROUND ME. THE EARTH, THE ELEMENTS, PEOPLE PLACES AND THINGS.

THIS ACTUAL LOVING EMOTION OF BEING CONNECTED

IS WHAT I CONSIDER THE FAMILY, THE WORLD, THE LOVE OF MY LIFE! IMAGINE LEARNING HOW TO PERFECT AN EXISTENCE WHEREIN ONE LOVES EVERYONE ANYTHING AND EVERYTHING WITH A CONSCIOUS KNOWLEDGE OF BEING CONNECTED TO EVERYTHING, AND IN THIS STATE WHOLE HEARTEDLY ATTRACTS ONE'S BLISS AND ONE'S JOY.

IN BEING REBORN INTO THE NEW ME I ALSO HAD TO BECOME REBORN IN THE RELATIONSHIPS I LEFT BEHIND, REBORN INTO A WORLD OF MY OWN CONSCIOUS CREATION DEFINED BY ME. HOW DOES ONE MAKE UP 30 YEARS? HOW DO I DESCRIBE 30 -50 YEARS OF THOUGHTS, EMOTIONS, FEELINGS AND EXPERIENCES? WITHIN THESE WRITINGS EXISTS AN OFFERING IN MY QUEST TO FIND MY WAY BACK TO MYSELF AND TO OTHERS.

IN CREATING THE NEW HEAVEN AND THE NEW EARTH

WITHIN MY PERSONAL EXPERIENCE I LOOK FORWARD TO SHARING EACH NEW EXPERIENCE WITH THE NEW ME. THE THOUGHTS AND FEELINGS I WRITE HERE ARE A PART OF MY HEALING, A PART OF MY INWARD GROWTH AND DEVELOPMENT. WITH EACH WORD WITH EACH PAGE I LOVINGLY CONTINUE CREATING THESE NEW EXPERIENCES AND MEMORIES AS ME, LLYANA, DEFINED BY ME AND GOVERNED BY ME.

Dad,

"We were in the car together with me in the driver's seat riding down some main road in America it seems. It was dusk, the light turning different shades just before getting dark. I happened to look out of my window and I noticed there was something strange happening in the sky. You noticed it immediately too. We stopped, got out of the car and looked up. What seemed to be stars, started to change formations and I realized that they were aircraft / UFO's. It was a sign of the times, a sign that a cycle had come to

an end".

I woke up from this dream realizing it was the first time I dreamed about you since I was nine... 33 years. Two hours later I heard from a third party that the leader of the cult I married into died the same morning I woke up from this dream. That same day one of my sons cut me off and expressed that he didn't have a mother because I posted, (on Face Book), the song from the movie the Wizard of Oz, with Judy Garland, "ding dong the witch is dead", he thought I was referring to the leader of the cult. I was referring to you tony. Ding dong you're dead to me.

I have carried you as a dead weight around with me for most of my life! Like a dark cloud hanging over everything I did, said, thought and felt. Every time I felt some semblance of happiness it was short lived because this cloud, you, were always on the horizon, always looming, always corrupting my perception of who I was / am and who I was / am meant to be. Does this make me strong or does this make me stupid and delusional? I am tired!!! My soul is tired!!! The blood that runs through my veins is tired of your dead weight!!! I am tired of existing outside of myself, outside of who I really am because of what you did to me. Because of what you put me through. Because of the death you imprinted on my soul, on my spirit, on my heart.

It has become such a part of me that to feel strong, to be happy and to find peace feels foreign to me. In fact everything feels foreign to me. More often than not I feel as if I am living outside of myself, outside of life, outside of the boundaries of gravity which would otherwise keep me grounded. How did your conscience allow you to destroy me from the inside out? How did your heart not realize that I died a slow death before I was even a teenager? How did you not realize that your behavior, your actions, your evil would have me living on the precipice of fear most of my adult life. Not fear of people, or situations. Not fear of danger. Not fear of circumstances, but fearing myself, fearing who I really am and who I want to be. Fearing my right to be happy, fearing my right to feel clean and pure. Fearing the goodness in me..... And DOUBT.....doubting myself constantly, doubting my thoughts, my dreams, my abilities, my capabilities.

How does some one come into this life which such a twisted moral compass? What did you get out of what you put me through? What did you gain? What was I at 6, 7, 8, 9, 10 years old supposed to gain from you corrupting my body, my mind and my soul. I tried to run away from it all. I tried to turn my back on my childhood and ended up repeating my childhood a thousand fold. Marrying into a cult wherein all the men where you. The leader of the cult was you. The penal system in the cult was you. The relationships were you. My marriage was you. I realize now that my entire adult life was about punishing myself for the sins of my childhood. Sins that only existed in my mind, according to how I was imprinted to perceive myself.

Always asking myself what did i do wrong and how can I improve myself? A never ending rhythm and cycle of never being satisfied with just being me! Just being ok with who I am at the moment. I have had thoughts of revenge. I have had fantasies of causing you pain. Not the revenge and pain like in the movies.

But your pain and suffering came by you having to admit that you did enjoy being "attracted" to me as a child. The pain of you having to admit that you liked it. The pain you will feel when you have to admit who you really are, and what you really are. There was no audience, no one but you and I. In these thoughts I didn't want to prove to the whole world that you were disgusting and evil. I wanted to prove to myself that I was right about you and that I hadn't made any of this up. No one believed me back then, so why should they believe me now? But I wanted to prove to myself that I wasn't crazy. I wanted you to suffer in having to admit that you are evil, that you are a monster. Just for my own clarity. So I could once and for all stop questioning myself, ABOUT EVERYTHING.

I want to hurt you, I want to make you suffer, I want to condemn you to a death like no other, but once again, fear. Fear that these thoughts will bring me bad karma. Fear that I will have to repeat this life over again because I had evil thoughts about you. Fear that these thoughts will destroy the good person i am working so hard to be in spite of feeling soulless most of the time. I wish I could change my life. I wish I could start over again as if none of this ever happened. I just wish I had a life wherein my cup didn't "runneth over" with pain, emptiness, longing, and fear of me. I want to live but don't know how. I want to be happy but don't know how. I want to feel free but don't know how. I want to flow downstream for once in my life instead of always swimming upstream.

I want the kaleidoscope of life to change colors so I see only the good in me. So I see only the colors that are not you. So I see only your nonexistence in every realm, in every dimension, in every universe, in every world. You never were, you never are, and you never will be....

Most of all..... I still want to hate you

I am so so so unhappy with myself and with life! Most of my time i spend being depressed, crying and just living life from my bed, pretending everything is ok but it is not. This has been going on for years. What got me through everyday was knowing my children needed me and I couldn't let them suffer (while they were growing up). I could in no way shape or form let them down, just because I was struggling. But now that everyone is grown I am surrounded by just me and my empty life. I find myself wondering if I would miss me if I wasn't here. Don't worry i am not planning to commit suicide, just sometimes I wish I could disappear and start over again without the horror and trauma of my childhood, without the horror and trauma of the "community", my marriage and just even living here in Israel. This shit goes way back and goes deep. But it keeps resurfacing in my life within my thoughts and within my soul. Not that i think about the past, I just feel like no matter what I do, where I go, or who I am with, no matter how much I laugh, there is always a dark cloud hanging over me waiting for the first opportunity to consume me if I give in. Feelings of being so hurt and so sad and so upset that no matter what I did nothing helped. Well that is me year after year after year after year. Not knowing what to do about it or who to turn to. Some have seen a peak of what I am living through but I hide it everyday so I won't seem weak or stupid.

I was told I need to have a plan. It was really good advice if only I could figure out what i really want. I for sure know what I don't want and what I don't like. I decided to really focus on coming up with a plan. It was suggested i do something here in Israel that is fun, or something i like to do, just to get me out of the house and my mind off of being sad and depressed. In trying to come up with some kind of plan, I realized that maybe the first step in me making some changes in my life is to find something that i absolutely love. This way my mind and my soul will be on what feels good to me and what I love instead of all the other bullshit. For such a long time I felt I was on a downward spiral that kept getter harder and harder to get out of. And at this point I HAVE TO do something about it. I just can't keep going on like this. I have wasted so many years being unhappy and depressed. I want to know what it feels like to be happy for once, to enjoy my life for once and to be able to look in the mirror and know that it was all worth it.

I found something I think I would love to do that just might be the first step in the door to attracting other things in my life that will free me up and make space for the happiness and fulfillment I have deprived myself of for so long. I decided I want to do a Skipper's course to be licensed to sail any kind of yacht, boat, sail boat, speed boat, etc, up to 50 meters long. It will get me out of the house, it will put me on the sea, which I love, it will give me a sense of freedom, which is a feeling that I am also looking for, and it will give me the opportunity to do something, finally, I absolutely love! And of course I can use this certification in the future for a family business, when I settle on "my island", or just for pleasure. Afterwards when and if the time is right I can continue on and become a licensed, certified skipper for yachts and boats as large as 100 tons if I choose to.

I just can't start this next phase of my life being the old, depressed unhappy me. I want to start this next phase of my life right, with a clean slate, a clean heart and with joy and happiness. I think of my children and I just feel so sorry their mother is not as strong as she would like to be. I am even sorrier I allowed my life to get to the point where I even have to expose myself as to how bad it really is. I would be so embarrassed to know that some one else knew the truth about what is really happening with me.

A year and a half ago I made a conscious decision to be homeless. It was one of the hardest decisions I've ever made! I was 100% disabled, couldn't work, bills up the gazoo, children to take care of, and rent to pay. I was burying myself deeper and deeper into a seemingly bottomless hole of debt. On top of all of this I was seriously depressed. I didn't know what to do or where to go. My mother gave me some really good advice. I always know when something is right when the first step in any given situation starts a chain reaction of everything flowing effortlessly and easily. My three youngest boys received scholarships for one of the top boarding schools in Israel. The second step was to pack up the house and give everything away. I thought about selling everything but remembered that everything had been given to me so I wanted to return the blessing for some one else. "*When you've been blessed, pass it on*", I hear Patty Labelle singing in my head.

For four years I couched surfed with friends, stayed in youth hostels or on my mothers couch. Everywhere I went my 3 youngest children were welcome whenever they got the weekend or a holiday off. At first it was exciting. No bills. I mean none. The money, time and energy helping whoever I stayed with didn't feel like a bill. It felt like an offering. I was able to invest more time and effort into my children. After the initial excitement and freedom of it all, it became old pretty quickly. But the underlying feeling of freedom was ever present.

In 2015 my two youngest boys literally kicked me out of Israel. They were still at the boarding school. Their exact words were, "*Ema we know you are unhappy and miserable here. We're older now, in a really good place, we have our two older brothers and*

Oma, (my mother), is we need anything. You have to go"! Thanks
to my oldest daughter specifically and my other children July
2015 I returned to America, Oregon, to be more specific.

The first six months were really good and extremely difficult due
to the inner transformations created by completely changing my
surroundings and outlook on everything. I did some traveling...
Costa Rica, San Francisco, Houston Texas, Oregon, Atlanta.
While journeying to theses different places I realized that I feel
the most free, the most blissful, the most joy and the most free of
any stress when I go someplace new, meet new people, learn
about diverse cultures and participate in these different from a
grass roots level with people, places and things from all walks of
life, from all religions, from all races and genders. It is this
connection I thrive on! It is the anticipation of learning something
new from any given circumstance, endeavor or sharing of souls.

Amidst all of this I still felt lost. Life was absolutely getting better and feeling better. But I still couldn't find or feel the real me. I soooo wanted a life I could be grateful for. I soooo wanted to wake up every morning with a true sincere gut wrenching feeling of gratitude and appreciation for everything in my life... for life itself. This mantra went out into the universe religiously from the time I left the "community".

September 5th 2016

What the fuck am I doing here? This has been one of the most scary, frightening, frustrating, awesomely wonderful experiences I have ever gone through. I am living in a shelter in downtown Seattle. Yes I am one of Seattle's homeless! The first day I arrived at the shelter I was in tears, trying to keep the heaving and sobbing down to a bare minimum so as not to expose how afraid I was. The woman at the front desk got up, walked around the counter and hugged me. She said, "*You are here now, you are aright, you're going to be ok, everything will work out*"! OMG what a woman!!! In fact for the last 4 days every one of the workers and volunteers at the shelter were been amazing!! Warm, compassionate, kind and accommodating as well as straight to the point and not taking any bullshit!

The shelter opens its doors to us at 8am. We come in, register, wait until 9am in order to sign up for a locker, make appointments for the showers and the washing machines. I have been blessed to be able to get into the shower at the 10m appointment. Then I repack my things and leave out and stay at the library until about 5pm. I have to check back in at the shelter before 6pm. I register agian in order to be assigned another shelter to spend the night. Thank god for Christians and Churches!!!! And I am supposed to be Jewish..... Thank God for Christianity and good Christians!!!! We wait until about 8:30pm in order to be informed as to where each group will be spending the night. The first night we stayed in a small complex of offices belonging to a church, super clean, super quiet. We laid thin mattresses on the floor, got clean one sheet and one blankets. Lights out was at 10:30pm, but most of us were already in the bed. Back up at 5:30 am the next morning and out the door by 6am. Drink cheap coffee at McDonalds until 8 am so I can use the restroom, back to the shelter and the cycle begins again.

All of the women in the shelter are exceptional in their own ways!!! Even the really crazy delusional fuckers are awesome. Women from all walks of life that are either, sick, disabled, and lonely with nowhere to go, no family or no one willing to help them. There are also women who have made being homeless a lifestyle. Women that talk to themselves or to people no one else can see. Some are very kind, helpful and docile, while others are downright rude and aggressive. But most of us learn early on who to leave alone and who not to get close to either because of their behavior or their hygiene.

I haven't laughed as much as I have these last 2 days compared to the last 4 months. Watching them make fun of some one else that they think is even more crazy than they are. Sometimes some of us think quietly..... What the fuck????!!!!! They offer breakfast lunch and dinner, and I have to say the vegetarian meals have been mostly tasty and surprisingly healthy. I made 3 new friends. A forty one year old ex heroine junky, a fifty five year old single lady and an American Korean thirty three year old that looks almost like a teenager. So thankful for these ladies in making my transition from one life to another so much more do-able!!!

I chose to see everything from this perspective because if I focused on the literal in my face reality of life in a shelter I would have crumbled.

There is a moment in everyday when i ask myself.... what the fuck Ilyana.... and the tears well up in my soul, in my heart but stop before they get to my eyes. I don't want to be weak or vulnerable! In each of these moments I want to throw my hands up, give up and go back to Israel. But I can't. I just can't. I have to see this through. I have to succeed in setting up a life for myself and my last 2 sons!!!! I can not fail at this!!! I keep putting it out into the universe.... THIS IS GOING TO TURN OUT BETTER THAN I COULD HAVE EVER EXPECTED, THOUGHT OR FELT.... this is my daily and hourly mantra. It has to be better at some point. I have to see this through, no matter how scary or how frustrating. At some point life has got to be good for me! Not just me making life better for everyone else. It's amazing how do-able it is for me to help everyone else but when it comes to me, my life and my happiness seems to be so hard. I look forward to the day I can sit in MY OWN front room, in MY OWN HOUSE!!!! That first day I am celebrating BY ROLLING A FAT ONE!!!!

GOD HELP ME HOLD ON!!!! GOD, JESUS, ALLAH, BUDDHA, THE UNIVERSE.... HHHHHEEEEEELLLLLLPPPPP! I need strength and endurance! Calling all angels!!!!! Today is labor day, the library is closed so i am sitting in star bucks, sipping my tea slowly so as to be able to stay here as long as possible until I have to go back to the shelter. The music is kinda loud and awesome. The employees are awesome.... happy, friendly and helpful!!!!

What happened next cold either be described as a fluke or the hand of God literally coming down and moving the pieces of my life. I witnessed it almost as if I was outside of my body. I had fined tuned my routine to include other churches to shower, dress, do laundry and just have a moment wherein I felt human, wherein I felt normal. These churches offered a clean environment, welcoming and warm environments and the staff were exceptional.

One such morning after wondering the streets of Seattle from 6 am until 7 am with all of my belongings, I finished at the showering, was getting ready to leave and the receptionist asked if I needed any other help? I inquired as to what kind of help they had available. She mentioned housing and I made an appointment with a case worker at the church. During our meeting she offered me a stack of applications for different housing solutions and apartments. She went through them with me. She came across one and stated that I would want to apply to this organization because it was a 1 hour ferry ride west of Seattle. All I heard was ferry. All I saw was me on the water on a boat. I grabbed this application and sailed to Bremerton WA the next morning.

The application was submitted to the county housing organization. I was informed there was a 34 year waiting list. I felt a nano second of despondence then thought to ask if there was a shelter in the area.

September 16th 2016 was the first day of the beginning of my new life and the first day I stepped foot into the shelter for women and children in Bremerton. Some would say I ended up here by a fluke, others would say it was the hand of God moving the pieces of my life in such a way so as to finally afford me the opportunity to put the finishing touches on the healing process I prayed and begged for, for many years.

Going through the Seattle homeless shelter system and at the risk of sounding ungrateful, I can only describe the day in day out physical reality as horrific. Even though I did have a roof over my head, ate twice a day, interacted with awesome staff, this experience was like something from a horror movie... Drugs, alcohol, filth, and the constant daily onslaught of aggression, confrontation, being cursed, theft and threats. All I could do was remain quiet, keep to myself and shut down in an effort to just make it through to the other end, what ever end that would be.

Everyday all day long I carried all of my belongings with me. Lockers were provided but no locks so I only left a few items I wasn't concerned about being stolen. The bathrooms and showers stayed dirty and were set up for monitoring purposes because of drugs and alcohol. In other words NO PRIVACY...AT ALL. I returned to the shelter by 6pm every evening to sign a list for somewhere to sleep. We waited until 8:30 pm and then travelled via two buses, with all of my belongings to sleep on a concrete floor on a very thin mat in the auditorium of a Cathedral.

After nightly arriving at the Cathedral we waited outside, rain or shine, to be admitted. All of my belongings were placed in plastic bags because of bed bug epidemics being allowed to take out what I slept in and toiletries. We lined up to get a mat, a sheet, and one cover. I used my sweater as a pillow. I went to bed while the other women had something to eat. I was just too tired to even be bothered. We were up again by 5:30 am and out of the door by 6am after having a small breakfast. The day shelter didn't open until 8am and my options were limited. I either walked the streets of Seattle, waited until 7am to be admitted to another church to take a shower in a clean environment and do some laundry, or sat at McDonalds drinking coffee because I had to purchase something in order to use their restroom. Oh yes, there was another church I went to instead of McDonalds where they offered a really good breakfast when I was really hungry. This was the daily cycle.

After years and years of an extremely difficult life.... an unhappy childhood due to an abusive father, (mentally, physically and emotionally), married into a religious cult in a foreign country, gave birth to 11 children, abandoned by the ex-husband when my youngest was 1 and my oldest was 15. Being a single mom to 11 children until they were grown... gradually piece by piece I shut down, emotionally, just to survive and make it through each day. When I arrived at the shelter in Bremerton, I was numb and hanging onto survival by a thread. By this time the only reaction I had any energy for, if provoked, was to fight back even if just verbally, in the hopes that some one anyone would or could catch me when I finally collapsed into nothingness.

The first day I met the assistant director of the shelter, I got into a big fight with her. I thought I was just defending myself, in actuality I had yet to discover I didn't have to fight or defend myself anymore. After this initial encounter I prayed... to the Universe, to God, to Jesus, to Allah, to Buddha... I knew within my soul I belonged here and couldn't allow myself to get in my own way. My encounter with her was the best thing that happened to me and for me. It was my wake up call. I was tired, I didn't want to fight for my life anymore, I couldn't any longer solely function in a defensive mode. I made the decision then and there that I would do what it took to make this work. I promised her from that day forward she would never have another problem from me. It was upward and onward from there.

The assistant director became in my eyes, the "*gate keeper*" for the shelter. There was structure, there were rules, a dress code, chores, rules of conduct and engagement, a standard for cleanliness for the House, personal hygiene and a daily regimen. She was there to make sure all of us, during a ninety day period, did our best to comply with the structure and philosophy of the shelter as a means to afford us the vision, desire, motivation, and inspiration to recreate our lives and successfully move on.

The director embodied the philosophy of her friend, who the shelter is named after, to materialization and fruition...A drug and alcohol free environment in which the mission is to ensure that low-income, displaced, and homeless women and children as well as those experiencing domestic violence were being afforded the opportunity to seek ways to achieve health, safety, and well-being for themselves and their families without the concern of food, shelter, and clothing.

She, the director became my case worker and succeeded in manifesting this creation in my life. Having a degree in psychology she also became my therapist. Her method of "*Down & Dirty*"... intensively getting to the core of the challenges and issues that brought me to where I was at the time... catapulted me out of a 30 year slump I had encased myself in. She even made me carry a tomato in a sealed bag around with me EVERYWHERE for more than 3 weeks as part of her program.

For years I looked for some one I could trust, some one I felt safe enough with to unfold and uncover the most vulnerable parts of my soul, feelings and thoughts. The director provided the arena wherein I was free and safe, for the first time in my life, to be able to say anything and everything without being judged, without feeling ashamed. Without having to be strong because that was what was required of me. I knew I was safe with her because she didn't ask me. Leann TOLD me... "*WE ARE DOING THIS*"! But she had me at... "*I won't leave you until it's finished*"...

The director and the assistant director were the "*dangerous duo*" that tagged teamed me throughout this process with the support of a board of directors that promotes, assists, and encourages the Georgia's House process of rehabilitation back into a successful life and or standard of living for women and children. During these 90 days I was housed, clothed, fed (mentally, spiritually, emotionally & of course plenty of food) in order to give me the opportunity, the respite, and the safety net to only focus on my growth, development, and success. Every week I was given a list of things to do. Whether it was going to the DSHS office, the Doctor, Social Security Office, Kitsap resource Center (KCR), etc., or just... "*Make sure you take some time out for yourself*" so you don't get overwhelmed or burnt out.

The person I was on that September 16th 2016 is not the same person I am now as a result of my time here. This entire experience, for me, can only be described as enlightening in every sense of the word. I am renewed, rejuvenated, and reborn. For some this may sound too good to be true. For others it may sound miraculous. Was it easy? Not always. Did I ever get discouraged? Sometimes. Did I ever want to run and hide again in the old me? Initially almost every day until I looked up one day and couldn't remember the last time I wanted to flee, have a drink or get high. Thank you!!!!

I very often still wonder what the fuck am I doing here? What is my purpose and does it really matter whether I have a well defined purpose or not. Who really cares what my purpose is? I DO. Who am I really, and why the fuck did I volunteer for this in depth personal illusion that I have imagined for myself? I so want to be free! Free of issues, free of insecurities, free from boredom, depression, frustration, and a mentality of lack.

I look at my children and am finally able to see movement, progress, personal goals being accomplished, and a family cohesiveness has returned after so much chaos and confusion. I think we really want the same thing. Our family back together again. Not necessarily living in the same location but definitely being on the same page as concerns family, acceptance, allowance, respect and dignity.

I look back over my life and think... "for what"? Between all of the information about conspiracies, secret societies, politricking politicians, warped society, warped people, warped organization, warped crimes, etc., etc. FOR WHAT? And then there are and my 11 children. What is our part in all of this? How do we fit in? How do we/I go about recreating something from seemingly nothing when there doesn't seem to be any precedence for creating the ultimate peace and utopia. Or is this just what I want and assume that everyone else wants it too.

I think about me and who I am. I can feel me, the extended version of me, the other 90% me that is not physical. It almost feels like the real me has to fit through a bottle neck in order to experience the physical me. So I have to squeeze tight in order to become one with the physical me. One would think that this bottle neck would only squeeze forth the best, the most positive and the sweetest parts but instead, along with the best of me being sqeezed through, also came the conditions wherein insecurity, self doubt and fear flourish as if my life is a petri dish. Am I the scientist then, experimenting unconsciously with this illusion called my life?

As I grew, as I learned, as I put into practice.... self determination... self destiny... self validation.... self appreciation... self respect... and taking on the responsibility and accountability of self empowerment... I understood more and more that the Law of Attraction and the Law of Allowance go hand in hand. I became more and more enthralled with openly, naively and naturally consolidating these two laws as the precedent and covenant for my life. My adulation and form of worship turned inward instead of outward. Loving the "god", source energy, universe, that perches on the epiface of all that is me...."*I am that I am*"... and... "*I will be that which I will be*", (literal translation of the Hebrew). All the while inextricably learning that everyone has their own path. Everyone comes under the auspices of the Law of Allowance. What works for me may not work for some one else. Who cares who the messenger is? DID YOU GET THE MESSAGE? I barely know what the purposes of my life experiences are. Who am I to determine what the life purpose of some one else's experiences are? Who am I to judge the race, the gender, the religion or sexual orientation of anyone else?

As I became more accepting of myself I also became more accepting and repsectful of other people's life paths, choices and self determination. As I became more at peace with myself, my surroundings became more peaceful. As my "why" became more clear the unwanted personal baggage disappeared and other people's baggage was just that…Other people's baggage. This about face from the external to the internal enhanced my compassion for others because I no longer sought to personally change them, their circumstances or their challenges. I only sought to love them more as I loved myself more.

My core value became everything to do with my emotional body.... my feeling self. IT HAS TO FEEL GOOD TO ME!!! Period! What I eat, think, read, watch, talk about, how I connect with people places and things... the conversations I have.... what I wear ad infinitum. Until I grow into, develop into, or am spiritually and and emotionally born again into something as good or better.

I began to grasp more and more that there is no destination. The journey is the destination. This concept, this perception of life of the journey alleviated so many fears and so much stress from my thoughts and from my life. If the journey is the destination then there is no time limit. There is no finality on results. There is no limitation on how, what, when, where or why, thereby allowing for the companion of eternity to remain tangible. Inaugurating itself into my life with glimpses, then moments, then seasons, inexorably speaking to me from the pulpit of source enegy in the language of the universe.

I learned to understand this language of the universe using my emotions to decipher the energy / message / understanding waiting for my approval and activation. Everything I felt became valid. Everything I thought became worthy. The consecration of my journey was knighted by choice and the determination to be free.

I have also been blessed to become a new and improved me. Some one that I have always wanted to be and didn't know how. Some one that I like and respect. Some one that likes and respects me and all of the layers of me. I no longer feel as if I have to hide any part of me from myself. I am learning how to be first on my list instead of last on everyone else's list. I am still trying to understand who I am, where I come from and what lead me to this day – to this life and where I am going. Who am I really? Thus I continue to write. It is like a cleansing. As I peal away the layers more is revealed and more becomes clear.

Everything that manifested in my life, without fail, was/is a result and a reflection of my thoughts and more specifically of my emotions. Imagine a maze of dominoes. Touching just one domino will set off a chain reaction knocking over all of the dominoes one by one as if a train ran through them. They can even fall in different directions and along different paths simultaneously. This is how life manifests. Once I chose life for the sake of my children my mind, soul, and emotions now had the space to be open to considering other reasons for living. Therefore, all I experienced, all that was manifested down to the lowest common denominator, even down to the dynamics that existed in relationships between people that were in my space, and seemingly had nothing to do with me, was a result of just one domino, one thought, one emotion. So at the end of the day what manifests always always comes back to me.

My perception of the world is interpreted through my past

experience, my wants, my desires, my biases and my knowledge of the world around me. As my experience and understanding of the nature of consciousness deepened, I came to see how much of my life was pointing to a new understanding of everything around me.

A new understanding of the choices standing before me, feeling joy and happiness or feeling fear and pain. Realizing and learning that choosing joy and happiness was not in conflict with who I am and where I am going.

THUNDEROUSLY WHISPERING

Talk to me thunderously whispering the echo of freedom calling to my soul, Attaching itself to the ever evolving spirit Of what is holy within me.

Cry with me silently welcoming The torrential waters reaching for my heart, Cleaving to the unlimited space Of what was once emptiness embedded upon me.

O, but for the yearning of wisdom's pedigree, Groomed and prepared as a bride, Pending, longing for the moment which pulsates In expectation of this next phase of life.

Walk with me carefully pondering, The intimacy of dreams entranced to my world, Of different realities ever enshrined amongst The temple of our true being.

Approach with me ultimately uniting, The various realms of gods within, Upon which our sanctification Belies the sacredness of eternity.

O, but for the necessity of understanding's domain, Brought forth on the wings of destiny.

CHAPTER IV

The God Realm

According to modern day scientists, humans only use 10% of

thier brains (neurological capacity). CHANGE THE

TERMINOLOGY. Use the word **CONSCIOUSNESS** instead of the word brain. Then you can say that: ***HUMANS USE ONLY 10% OF THEIR CONSCIOUSNESS!!!*** Therefore there is another 90% of your consciousness you are not aware of, not using, or may not know how to use.

Humanity has time and again looked outside of itself for a savior, a messiah, a redeemer and / or a god. This is because we have been relying on the 10% of our consciousness in order to live according to the dictates of what has been passed on to a person by other people. Through the ages individuals have come along that may have known how to use 11%, or 12% maybe even 15% and have been looked upon as gods, messiahs or redeemers.

The bottom line is the other 90% you are not using or may not know how to use, is in actuality GOD. So the focus should be to turn inwards and activate the 90% or activate the God factor within yourself, thereby becoming a conscious Creator and creating your own destiny and the world you want to live in.

When you begin to activate this other 90% you no longer need permission or validation for anything or from anyone because you are in tune with Universal Law and the entire Creation will stand as your witness and strength.

How then do you know if you are on the right path? For so long we have looked for a god outside of ourselves to guide us and determine whether we are doing the right thing or not. However, once you turn inwards, and begin to activate and learn about the other 90% that is you, your entire system of worship has to be inward. Worship the Yah / God / Christ / Universe that is within you...the God that is you. You will know if you are on the right path by how happy you are and by how good you feel. It is just that simple!!!

How do you become acquainted with and activate the God factor within you...the God factor that is you, the other 90% of your consciousness? Just be aware it is there and that you want to know more. The necessary information will come to you. Use your happiness as the marker in your life to determine how well you are doing. Can I expand my consciousness to encompass the process that lies just beyond my grasp, the consciousness which dwells within the 90% realm of existence?

The focus of energy that holds and balances the creations doesn't require doesn't require effort. The idea of power usually translates as force. Since thought attracts thought, I brought to myself the the experience of effort, force, and power. It is not the gravitational field that ties me to this reality, to this life, it is my consciousness.

Cooperation is natural as long as the need to control and have power over everyting and everyone is absent. The need to control is a learned trait that becomes habitual through practice. We have been influenced to change what is present rather than to desire something entirely and completely new. You can't change the old but you can create the new. Change has been used before but it did not help completely. Within the right choice of focus lies my salvation. Subtle energy is powerful and the most powerful energy is subtle. I learned how not to allow myself to dwell on the horrors of what was happening and turned my thoughts to what it is I would prefer to experience.

It was my individual inner change that conquered forces pursuing control of my very essence of self awareness. It was easier to allow the seduction of my five senses into believing this is all there is. Once I was exposed to this mind altering mind, suppressing process it lulled me into relaxing. The creative self contemplating portions of my awareness were being shut down. The more my experiences repeated themselves the more it became an addiction. I was lulled into a dream state by the distraction of my consciousness awareness in order to separate me from my self aware state.

In order to use my energies wisely in my spiritual path, I had to try to connect with this energy / force within me, my own self awareness. I had to retrieve my soul and all of its superior qualities. When everything is open and activated it creates a personal dwelling place for my, "*I AM THAT I AM*", (*I will be that which I will be*), here on earth. It is the place from which I can function to co-create heaven on earth within my soul. It is my base of operations.

Everything that manifested in my life, without fail, was/is a result and a reflection of my thoughts and more specifically of my emotions. Imagine a maze of dominoes. Touching just one domino will set off a chain reaction knocking over all of the dominoes one by one as if a train ran through them. They can even fall in different directions and along different paths simultaneously. This is how life manifests. Therefore, all that I experienced, all that was manifested down to the lowest common denominator, even down to the dynamics that existed in relationships between people that were in my personl space, with seemingly nothing to do with me, were a result of just one domino, one thought, one emotion. So at the end of the day what manifests always always comes back to me.

My perception of the world is interpreted through my past experience, my wants, my desires, my biases and my knowledge of the world around me. As my experience and understanding of the nature of consciousness deepened, I came to see how much of my life was pointing to a new understanding of everything around me. A new understanding of the choices that stood before me; feeling joy and happiness or feeling fear and pain. And realizing and learning that choosing joy and happiness was not in conflict with whom I am and where I am going.

Something very interesting happened to me the other day. For the first time in my life I looked into the mirror and saw and felt hope. Hope in myself. Hope that I can actually do this. Hope that one day and maybe one day soon I will see the beauty in me. I saw a glimpse of the pretty girl I always wanted to see but never could. How did this come about? What brought this on?

Well…after twenty-four years I plucked my eyebrows again. I look completely different. I saw the beginning stages of how I always wanted to look. Of how I used to look and didn't even know it. Doing this was the second most important thing I have done for myself that has helped me to feel like me again. The first was piercing my nose. When I looked in the mirror – something woke up inside of me that continues to remain determined to do whatever it takes in order to feel good about myself, to feel pretty, to feel whole again.

I decided to pierce my nose after much stressing and turmoil over this decision. For many years I wanted a nose ring. I was so scared. I was afraid that I would be seen as wicked and evil in the eyes of Yah, in the eyes of the "community", that they would disown me. I was literally shaking and sweating when I sat down in the store that day. But I just had to do this. I had to do something for me. I finally had to do something that "*I*" wanted to do because "*I*" wanted to do it. I just prayed Yah would understand and have mercy on my wicked soul. Well…nothing happened. Lightening didn't strike me, my heart didn't stop and the ground didn't open up and swallow me and I finally had a nose ring.

In continuing to discover who I am I allowed myself to take certain liberties I would never have taken in the past. I also allowed some liberties as concerns my children. During the twenty-two years I lived in the "community", I was very strict and very zealous about keeping and following all of the rules and guidelines and doctrine of the *"Kingdom"*. I fully believed in it and didn't just preach it but lived it. After leaving I allowed myself freedom to assess what was really me and what wasn't. Liberties such as eating potato chips, falafels – sometimes eating something on the Shabbat, (fasting on the Shabbat was one of the pillars of the "community").

I found that eventually a lot of what I was doing would cease. I feel better without them. They are not a part of me. Nor do I need them. But I needed this time, time away from prying eyes so I could judge for myself and discover for myself the Yah / God within me. The Yah / God in me I was learning to consciously activate and affect my everyday life and my daily thoughts.

There is a school of thought within some religions and within some types of consciousness which believe we must suffer in order to attain oneness with God, we must suffer in order to overcome our baser selves. I believe we must suffer only in order to finally come to the conclusion we don't ever have to suffer again in life! Not physically, not financially, not emotionally, not spiritually, not in any way shape or form! In allowing myself to suffer, whether consciously or unconsciously, I started a chain reaction giving others the right to make me suffer, the right to help me suffer. In so doing I am handing over my right to conscious self-destiny and self-control. This same chain reaction continues onto my children who by way of example will grow up and repeat history. Is this then the legacy I would choose to leave them…suffering and misery?

I want my children to know they have a choice. They can choose life…they can choose to be truly free…they can choose to have control over their own destiny and then govern that destiny. They can choose joy and happiness. In turn each one of them can show some one else what they have learned thereby starting a chain reaction of their own, a pro-life, pro-creation, pro-happiness chain reaction.

We live in a world of opposites, up/down, hot/cold, dark/light, good/evil, so whatever is present in your life its exact opposite has to exist in the same space or in close proximity. Therefore the only land of captivity or the land of the free is the land of your soul. Is my soul keeping me captive or freeing me.

People often talk about racism, injustice, cruelty, religious and intolerance just to name a few... but I am proud of humanity and all we've accomplished. Today we can go to a restaurant, a mall, a concert an event and co mingle with people from other cultures, races, religions, and upbringings as if this is the way it has always been. How long ago was slavery an institutionalized way of life? How long ago were women not allowed to vote? How long ago did black people as a whole have to enter through the back or another entrance, or sit in the back of the bus? How many more people are becoming healthy, conscious, vegetarians, exercising and turning towards, using "greener" alternatives for their homes, neighborhoods, society, the planet? How much more information is available to us today in order to better ourselves as individuals, as families, as a society as a planet? More and more that I can see. Yes the other negative views and lifestyles still exist, but so the fuck what! Me, I just feel better when I focus on what is so good about people, and things.

Somebody mentioned it was amazing that I had 8 children out of 11 with driver's licenses, and this was unheard of in the "kingdom". I really thought about this and one thought led to another as the children's successes, individually and as a working functioning loving unit, flashed before me like a virtual slide show. I realized I finally made it over the hump, past the hard part and now there are only 3 younger children to inspire. The other 8 were all on their way and are continuing to develop a system wherein they support, love and help one another/themselves, and finally this no longer was something on my plate that I had to deal with or worry about. HOLY SHIT WHAT A LOAD OFF!!! I at that very moment felt so accomplished!!! WE DID IT!!!

These revelations also helped me to accept that I deserve the best as well. I deserve to be opulent, free, at peace and at ease. Every season I have a song or an affirmation that carries me throughout the trying times, (a season can last as long or as short as needed). Last season it was a song by Bob Dylan,

"Clowns to the left of me, jokers to the right, here I am...Stuck in the middle with you"

Every time some bullshit or bullshitter would cross my path, I would hum or sing this song to myself. It kept me on an even keel. This season my affirmation has been and still is...

MY LIFE IS EFFORTLESSLY BLISSFULL AND

BLISSFULLY EFFORTLESS!!!

Everything that I/we have done this past month was achieved on sheer faith and trust in universal law, in each other and in ourselves. I have learned there is no such thing as "no", "impossible", "can't be done" etc. I heard government officials tell me no, it's impossible, it can't be done. I then watched as universal law lined up for me all the things others said were impossible, and within one day I had my passport, permission to leave Israel, and was on a plane to Atlanta and Portland. And it can only get better. IT JUST FEELS SO MUCH BETTER TO FEEL BETTER!!!

I decided to Photoshop all of my pictures because I have to tell a new story. It doesn't feel good living inside of the outer shell of me, the me I created to please others. Pleasing my children, pleasing my friends, pleasing whoever. One of the greatest revelations of all was coming to the conclusion that I am not apologizing anymore nor will I feel guilty about my actions or the way to becoming me again. Not me the mother, me the daughter, me the wife, me the friend etc. BUT ME...who I really am, what I really feel! My transition into ME was more difficult for some of the children than others. I no longer was allowing myself to be as involved with the children, as a mother /parent. However I was involved as a person, as a co-existing adult, which in turn placed them in a position to have to grow up some more too!!! In the process I am learning how to accept me as an adult, as an individual, as a person.

After perusing my/our accomplishments, and 8 children being well on their way with their lives, it also hit me... I only have 3 minors left. I did the math. I have less than 25% more to do as concerns raising the children. I can now more and more finally focus on me, who I really am, what I really like, what I really want to do etc. So what do I want the most?

After having lived through being raised by an incestuous

pedophile loco tyrant, occult practicing, wanna be wizard, marrying into a cult, being pregnant every year for 16 years, having 11 children, being a single mom of 11 children since my oldest was 15 and the youngest was 1 year old; having to go house to house begging for food for 11 children, growing vegetables in order to feed them, and then getting chastised by the cult leaders for using water to grow the food. Heating water on the stove in order to bathe everyone, washing everyone's cloths by hand because we didn't have a washing machine; sewing all of our clothing, making everything from scratch; the leadership of the cult trying to literally kill me mentally physically spiritually. Children that at one time or another held me accountable and responsible for every negative deed or seed that was planted in their minds in an effort to brainwash them against me. Being followed, even coming into my home and looking through my things in my absence. Having my children spying on me unbeknownst to them that they were actually spying. Being estranged from my family, etc....what do I want the most?

A LIFE OF LEISURE, PLEASURE, OPULENCE, A DISPOSABLE INCOME, BLISS, SUCCESS, EFFORTLESSNESS, AND AN AWESOME FUCKING SOCIAL LIFE!!!

"Just sayin". Finally coming back into my own feels good! My own what?

OWN: of, pertaining to, or belonging to oneself or itself (usually used after a possessive to emphasize the idea of ownership, interest, or relation conveyed by the possessive); (used as an intensifier to indicate oneself as the sole agent of some activity or action, preceded by a possessive; /browse/own).
http://dictionary.reference.com

My own... so what do I own? Do I own my life? DO I own my children? Do I own anything at all? OWN, something that belongs to me! So what essentially belongs to me? Does my body belong to me? Does my mind belong to me? According to religion, I belong to "God", so therefore "he/she" must own me. Am I then a slave? A slave to "God", a slave to my body, a slave to society, a slave to my mind? What do I really own? What really belongs to me? If my body truly belongs to me then I should be able to decide what I want, how and when I want it, including physical characteristics, health and well being, and even death. If my body belongs to me then I should

be able to decide if it should die or not, even when. If I do not possess this type of influence or power over my body then I am a slave to it! It rules me not I rule it. The same can be said for everything else.

If I am a slave to "everything" then my whole life is fate or destiny or both and I have no say so in it. I am just a chess piece being moved around the board by other players. Whether the players are my body, society, my children, people I meet and so on. Maybe I should just wing it being that I don't own anything and nothing belongs to me? Not even me belongs to me. Or maybe I have these thoughts because I am a control freak and have no clue how to let go?

After all of this thinking, not just here on paper but through out my life, I wonder about what is a slave truly? Slave = pawn = appliance; appliance meaning an instrument, apparatus, or device for a particular purpose or use. So if I am a slave/pawn/appliance for anything or anyone other than myself how do I regroup, re-empower, recharge, rejuvenate, and re-apply (appliance) for self ownership? Is this even possible today? If being a slave ultimately makes me an appliance for a particular purpose then who decides what the/my purpose is? THE MATRIX????????????? lol

Purpose: the reason for which something exists or is done, made, used, an intended or desired result; end; aim; goal. Determination, resoluteness. The subject in hand; the point at issue, practical result, effect, or advantage: to act to good purpose.

Did I volunteer to be an appliance for some one or something else's agenda? I don't remember receiving the memo! So if I didn't volunteer how did I get into the predicament wherein something or someone else owns me? And if this was all put into place as a result of 2000 years of societal complacency how do I purpose myself for my "*own purposes*"? How do I once again take ownership of me? Or do I already have ownership and just became slave-like because this was unconsciously expected of me?

I just want to be me, be safe, be happy, be successful, be prosperous and be free. I guess this is really what i am looking for!!! THE FREEDOM TO BE ME, DO ME, AND APPLY (appliance) ME TO ANY GIVEN CIRCUMSTANCE WITH THE ULTIMATE GOAL OF BEING JOYFUL and in so doing open the door, hold the door open or point to the door wherein others may find personal salvation according to the dictates of their quest for freedom and fascination/joy/ happiness with themselves first and foremost and life.

JUST WANNABE ME AND BE FASCINATED WITH ME AND WITH LIFE!!!!!

The question for me is WHY!? Why am I here? Why live the life I've lived? Why make the choices I have made? Why endure the things I have endured? Why think the thoughts I have thought? I lean more towards the esoteric, spiritual, nonphysical world of energy. So far in my life I have not found anything that makes me feel as good, as empowered, as balanced and as joyful as the immediate physical manifestation of the esoteric, spiritual, nonphysical in my personal physical reality.

My personal physical reality being my body, the physical outward fleshly manifestation, in this realm, of me. Not necessarily all of me, but me nevertheless. When I feel good, empowered, balanced and joyful my physical body just feels good. It is as if my physical body is the BAROMETER, the BRIDGE between the nonphysical and the physical. In conducting my life with this in mind, if I pay close attention to my body, if I feel/listen to my body, it puts me in the position of being able to create my personal physical and nonphysical reality according to how my body feels. Comfortable versus uncomfortable, healthy versus unhealthy, satisfied versus insatiable, the list goes on.

I am learning and practicing to READ the BOOK OF LIFE that is my body. After all, this is a bio-organic mechanism, super computer, and tool that I was given, or chose, in order to exist in this physical reality as me. If my body feels good (from within and without) then I know I am on the right path. I am not talking about immediate gratification and then afterwards feeling regret. I am talking about physically feeling good, empowered, balanced and my body rejoicing on a soul level. Here comes the question again...

WHY? Eons and eons of processes, intent, and purpose all in order for me to be here now. For you to be here now. Right here, right now at this very moment. After all we experienced, after all we witnessed, and after all we went through to be here at this very moment in order to do what? It is not so much that I want to or need to figure out every single detail but I seek an understanding. DIDN'T "GOD" TELL SOLOMON THAT "*IN ALL YOUR SEEKING SEEK YE AN UNDERSTANDING*"...

If life is an illusion and every single person here has their own personal illusion that mingles with other's illusions do I not then have the ability or even obligation to become a conscious creator if such a wonderful tool was/is being given to each and everyone of us. I have this awesome tool I can physically, mentally, emotionally and spiritually enjoy and the sky is the limit. But WHY!? Why even have this tool, this gift. Why give some one a magic wand to with as they please?

I don't fuckin know!!! All I know is I would rather feel good than feel bad. I would rather get along with everyone than fight with everyone. I would rather be healthy then be sick. I would rather live in peace then go to war. And I have this gift this tool that exists for me with its seemingly underlying purpose to CREATE/MANIFEST any type of illusion that I want and it does so whether I am conscious I am doing this or not.

Do I then go about trying to fix everything on the planet? Do I go about helping the poor, the sick, the tired and the weary? WTF I feel like a first grader studying the universe and universal processes/LAW. It is overwhelming and this does not feel good to me, to my body. What then can I do with this gift/tool that feels good to me too! If this is my illusion then it starts with me. And if our illusions are the physical manifestation of "energy"/"GOD"/the universe according to how we think and feel then I want to feel good too. I have to feel good first. This good feeling ripples out and ATTACHES to everything else.

How is this good feeling physically manifested instantaneously? How does this feeling of empowerment, balance and joy physically manifest itself instantaneously in my body in such a way that it ripples out into my illusion to create my personal reality? Via a chemical reaction. Every thought, every feeling manifests itself as a chemical reaction in my physical body. WHYYYYY???

Maybe my physical body is the barometer, the bridge between the physical and the nonphysical, it therefore is also an antennae sending out a vibration/sound/word ("*and the word was with GOD and the word was GOD...*"),or receiving one. This vibration being the chemical reaction that is taking place in my body as a result of my thoughts and feelings.

We have it whether we want it or not. It works 24/7 whether we want it to or not. It manifests whether we are conscious of what we manifest or not. It is the difference between going downhill or uphill. Flowing downstream or upstream, looking at the glass and debating whether it is half full or half empty, when in reality (for lack of a better word), "my cup runneth over"!

My body, is my personal bio-organic super computer,

mechanism, vehicle for manifestation in this illusion of anything I want or need. Is my purpose to bring joy or its opposite, love or its opposite, empowerment or its opposite? If my purpose is to manifest love, joy empowerment balance etc., then it has to start with even the most minute chemical reaction within me to ensure the continuous rippling out effect of this / my personal reality / illusion.

It feels like exercising to me. Once I get out of the cycle of exercising regularly it is hard for me to take those first few steps to get back into being in the cycle of exercising. Once I am in the cycle however, it alsmost becomes ritualistic. I still may not want to exercise, I still may not want to get out of bed or stop what I am doing but my body is in the cycle now and actually physically gives me the push to continue on each day. Then afterwards comes the feeling of empowerment, joy and balance.

When I have been out of cycle, whether it be a day or a year, of doing what makes me feel joyful, happy, positive, life becomes difficult, at times even extremely difficult to get back on track. When I get tired of feeling bad and seeing it manifest this energy even minutely in my life / illusion and the ripple effect it has on seemingly inconsequential things in other peoples lives that are touched by the ripple, I wake up. It literally feels as if a veil is lifted from my eyes and everything looks and feels clearer and lighter. I have been blessed to get back in tune with me... the 10% and the 90%... step by step, moment by moment, and percentage by percentage.

I read once that when we ELIMINATE fear and hope, we can then manifest from a platform of love. What is love? I mean really... WTF is LOVE". Love your brother, love your enemy, love your husband, wife, children etc., etc... Love for me is passion, passionate about love, about life, about a beautiful tree, a child, a car. In the realm of GOD/THE UNIVERSE is love all the same? Or is it just a human emotion. Can I hug a tree and feel love for it as I would for my child? Can I love the people that built the house I live in even though I don't know them and have never seen them? Can I love everything and everybody as I would my child, or my lover?

If everything is an outward physical manifestation, expression of me then it would stand to reason if I really wanted to love as described above then I would have to find something in everyone and everything that I could love in this manner, including myself. It would also seem to be true that as time goes on everything and everyone in my life/illusion would mirror this same love in some way shape or form.

In this same process I learn, practice, and become skilled in creating a conscious chemical reaction/life/illusion/world that inwardly and outwardly reflects finding the inner space to love everything and everybody and everything and everybody loves me. The outer world and it's dynamics no matter how far removed it may seem mentally, intellectually, culturally or geographically, whether a world of peace or a world of turmoil, is a reflection of the outward ripples/chain reactions of that one inner chemical reaction that acquired enough momentum via other like minded chemical reactions.

I feel my real life at my finger tips crawling up my arm like in the movie "The Matrix", when Neo saw his arm turning into a liquid silvery substance instead of the physical arm that he was used to seeing.. "*What the mind believes the eyes see*".

What are thoughts? Where do they come from? Where do they go? Do they come from the brain or the mind and is there a difference? My thoughts feel or seem like they come from inside of me. I don't read thoughts, nor do I see or feel them outside of me. I feel and see my thoughts from the inside and they present themselves as images. These IMAGES, (thoughts), display themselves across the screen of the Abyss of my internal and eternal self. I don't know how to describe it any other way... IMAGES DISPLAYED ACROSS THE SCREEN OF THE ABYSS OF MY INTERNAL AND ETERNAL SELF. These thoughts/images, if what I see and feel is CORRECT, come from the nonphysical rather than from the physical, from the nonphysical 90% of me, rather than the physical 10% of me. This being said, it then becomes apparent to me that, via the PROCESS of reconnecting with the other nonphysical 90% of me I can now consciously exist within the realm wherein I actively CHOOSE or LOCATE the IMAGES / thoughts according to the desired physical outcome in this the physical 10% realm.

Is this a continuous constant ride with no bumps no turns? Depends on what the individual attracts to themselves. I have succeeded in attracting the physical manifestation of the images that I carried with me that came as a result of how I translated my childhood experiences. Now, I am learning how to speak and understand the language of the universe wherein no translation is necessary. This universal language EXISTS within this REALM of images that we have projected on our very own screen of physical life. The question therefore stands before me..., "*Do I want to act in the movie according to a script or do I want to direct/produce/finance/ write/own this movie, this illusion*"?

Does this require me to exist in "la la land"? Uh yeah...for me it does!!! I ABSOLUTELY LOVE LA LA LAND!!! LA LA LAND IS THE PLACE WHERE I PRACTICE GOING REGULARLY! Does this make me irresponsible? No, I still hold up my "earthly" responsibilities, but I am learning to EXIST in a realm wherein I can create, recreate, tweak, twist and change my mind/thoughts/images as often as I want, how I want until I get it right. Until I feel good. Until I feel joy and bliss. Not having money for a bill and worrying about it versus the same situation and thinking about traveling someplace new. Meeting interesting people, envisioning my new home, WATCHING IMAGES DISPLAYED ACROSS THE SCREEN OF THE ABYSS OF MY INTERNAL AND ETERNAL SELF, just feels so much better.

I have noticed in my life that the more I practice this not only does it become easier but if I can do it 1x I can do it 2x. If I can do it 2x I can do it 4x. If I can do it 4x I can dot 16x and so on, reminds me of the FIBERNUCCI CODE. Until it becomes innate. In practicing and living this philosophy/way of life, the times I get depressed or overwhelmed are shorter and less severe. I could complain about finances, people, or situations, but why when I can just relax and think of something that just really makes me feel joyous and blissful, whatever that may be. I am then immediately transported to THE SCREEN OF MY INTERNAL AND ETERNAL SELF. Just being able to exist there even if just for a moment and feel joy rippling out to any and all given situations I may be dealing with in my external physical, 10% realm of this life.

Where do I go from here? Knowing this, practicing this, and learning to reconnect with me the real me... what do I want, what do I absolutely love, what makes me feel good? Questions that until 10 years ago I didn't know I had the right to choose let alone think about. I slowly succeeded in transforming my entire life, my every waking moment, into one of serving, helping, inspiring and motivating everyone but me. Not only did I forget me but I lost me and literally had to start over from scratch. All the way down to what do "I" like to eat? What do "I" like to wear, what makes "ME" feel joyful, healthy and prosperous? I once told some one that as a result of the life I had attracted my heart wasn't broken it was totally pulverized into nothing and the only way I could go on was to recreate a new heart, new lungs and other internal organs. In so doing there was no place for the past.

THIS would REQUIRE new images, (thoughts), new memories to look back on so as not to continue to make reference to what I don't want, (the past), as a part of any conversation.

I don't remember me. I am a stranger to my eyes? Looking back the past feels like a movie I sort of kind of remember, but not really... and my childhood, as if from another planet or something that happened to some one else. The past doesn't exist anymore, the future hasn't happened yet, and the only thing that exists is the present, the now.....? Who am I now? Who am I really? The true me? I know what I am good at, I know what I love and like, I know what makes me feel good. Does this define me? Is this all of me? I inately feel I am not just this body, (this "*coat(s) of skin*"). If this physical world is only 10% of me then where is the rest of me? Who or what is this rest of me?

Maybe it is all about the connection between the two, the bridge, and the wormhole? Isn't there more and more scientific evidence that this is an electrical universe? Isn't electricity all about CONNECTIONS? How do I know what this connection is and how does it manifest itself in my life? How do I measure what is real, what belongs to the real me? The 10% + 90% = 100% me? I innately feel that for me the measuring rod is how absolutely joyful or blissful I feel, how good I feel when I connect.

What do I feel connected to, passionately, with such a feeling of joy that I could just burst? I am passionate about nature, (nature for me is a perfect vibration), about the elements, being able to more and more, see, feel, and discover something wonderful in everything and everyone whose journeys crosses with my journey. Part of the process of life is to be able to love everyone and everything as just love. For instance I am absolutely in love with my children, or my lover, spouse, soul mate, etc. But am I able to have this same type of love for, not emotional(ism), but pure love for my neighbor for the people that collect the garbage every morning. For some one or something that is different from me or the opposite of me?

Can I love the earth, the fauna, flora, the beasts of the field? If this is an electrical universe, a world of energy then everything is a result of the dynamics of the vibrational connection I ADD to the planetary consciousness? It just seems logical to me that love feels so much better than fear, anger, and pain.

I can honestly confess that initially this path, this mindset was extraordinarily difficult for me. I was not the aggressive type that lashed out. I was the type that would take it all in and unconsciously punish myself because of the fear, anger, and pain. Most of the time it was just easier to lull myself back into focusing on what hurt, what made me angry, what I feared therein focusing on what I didn't want.

Having an addictive personality was addictive! As a means to feel better I decided to change my addictions. My addiction for emotional/boredom eating versus eating healthy. Absolutely hands down loving being a couch potato in front of the TV or the computer versus loving to come home after a vey productive day. A physical workout, shower, put on something really comfortable and then lounge in front of the computer or tv.

For me it is a win/win situation! I can have the pie and eat it too. (By the way... who the hell came up with... "*She wants the pie and wants to eat it too*"? Why in the fuck would I bake a pie and not eat it)? Anyway... It will be a raw fruit pie...very healthy! Along the way I can tweak it, fine tune it, or change it.

One of my children asked what is "GOD"? The diversity of being raised Jewish, attending born again Christian and Baptist churches, embodying the characteristics of a Hebrew Israelite and growing from being religious to being spiritual made me want to give my children a well rounded answer that would assist them on their personal path to finding out their own personal answer to this question. I replied that it was simple math. $1 + 1 = 2$ or $1 - 1 = 0$. In other words I can choose to focus on the terrible things that go on, the news, the wars, the end of the world scenarios, or I can focus on new beginnings. I can focus on the love that is not only needed but is ever present. I can focus on deficit and lack. Or I can focus on abundance and wealth.

I choose to exist if only for the reason that IT JUST PLAIN FEELS BETTER TO FEEL BETTER. More happiness, more tranquility, more daily interactions whether personal, momentary, official business. Anything and everything seemingly inconsequential or miscellaneous.

I can focus on the tragedies of my African American, Jewish, and the femanine heratiges and atrocities, to name a few. Or I can really appreciate, and be proud of everyone when I sit in a restaurant eating breakfast with my daughter and the place is packed with people waiting to be seated. Not only were the clientele diverse, Caucasian, African American, Hispanic, Asian, African... the entire staff was as diverse. Everyone seemed to enjoy themselves, everyone was polite, and people interacted table to table. The staff was friendly and professional with everyone. I sat there and thought this couldn't have happened 200, 100, 60 years ago. Even if there were people that had a problem with it they had enough sense and home training to act with the same respect and friendliness as everyone else.

At that very moment I was so proud! I was so proud of humanity, of everyone in that room. In that very moment I intended that everyone just carry and relish if even unconsciously, this joy, this blissful feeling, this moment of feeling so blessed. Silently I asked that everyone within the restaurant be blessed in some extraordinary way, whether financial, health, relationship etc., to lessen their suffering in anyway and rippling out in the best most joyous way possible. What seemed like a journey was in actuality a twinkle in time within time/space reality. In that moment, in that connection it felt like eternity it felt timeless.

This is where I feel the most free! Where I feel at home! It is in these moments where the mirror is me. I CAN SEE ME, I CAN FEEL ME,I CAN BE ME. From this vantage point into my soul I REALIZE that my journey is an out ward expression of me as well as an inward expression of me. Like the ying yang symbol. A VANTAGE POINT from physical eyes versus a VANTAGE POINT, from the soul, from within the connection, from within this realm would logically be different. One being the vantage point of pawn, versus the person moving the pieces. If we all have this innate gift, whether we know it or not or like it or not, to what end? For what?

YOU DON'T MEET MORE THAN YOU CREATE... David Wilcock

"I HAVE GIVEN UP ON GIVING UP"! A statement made by Elijah the original vampire in the television series "The

Originals". Wow what a statement!!! I have given up on giving up. This so speaks to me. Giving up has been a thought many times but never an option. Give up then what. Leave everything and everyone else behind so I have to come back around again and start over. I don't think so!

I am feeling more and more like me. How does me feel. I feel good from the inside out. I feel warmth from the inside out that just purrs, a feeling that when I focus on it, it makes me smile from ear to ear, or makes me smile, mischievously to myself. As if I am part of an inside secret between me myself and I.

So what is this secret, this inside joke? That I just plain feel awesome. Secret not being sneaky or slick, but the secret that I have finally realized I have the right to feel this good. I have the right to feel this pleased with myself. I have the right to look in the mirror and love what I see. I have the right to love being me. The way I dress the way I eat, the way I talk, the way I get pissed the fuck off! Wow, so is this normal, does every female go through this at my age and development?

My entire adult life as well as most of my childhood I have always taken care of others and have felt responsible and accountable for others. Now it is finally coming to me and I am finally at the time of my life wherein I can invest more and more time into doing me, being me, and living me. AND I FUCKIN LOVE IT!!!!!!!!!! I am not the president of a country, nor do I own a business, or run an organization. At the moment I don't even have a job so to speak because all of these years I have been a stay at home mom. I finally am able to more and more see and feel glimpses of how awesome I can and should feel. I finally feel like I got that "A", that 100%, now all I have to do is keep it.

The best thing about keeping an "A" is the only requirement is to continue to find my bliss. I also realize that my bliss, after all I have been through and after all of these years, is me. Discovering me, learning me, getting used to me, trusting me, having confidence in me, and allowing me! Through all of this discovery, and life lessons, on this journey, I realized I love me and like me more and more. This feeling of loving and liking me feels so much more awesome then looking for that same approval / validation from people, places and things outside of myself, outside of my soul, outside of my spirit. It is so much more empowering when you can love, like approve and validate yourself!

Is this then what all of this life shit is about? To come full circle, look in the mirror, and love me, all of me. WHAT A FUCKIN TRIP, a long ass trip at that. Coming full circle back to me.

I look at my children and see them setting up their lives in order to establish a firm foundation for their own individual futures. And now I can finally do the same for myself as an individual, not as a mother, a wife, an auntie, a grandmother. As an ADULT. I am now, in my early fifties doing what my children and most other people do in their 20's and 30's. Is it scary, and overwhelming? Sometimes it feels like a total mind fuck. But then I think about everything that I have learned on this journey about life, about me and instead of looking at the glass as either half empty or half full, I am so grateful and relieved that *"my cup runneth over"*. And I so prefer to go through life, even if I have to start over from scratch with a full cup, then not even knowing or realizing that I have a right to drink from this cup forever and ever or that there is even a cup in the first place.

Can this reaching out to one another be done in the midst of multiplied sorrow, oppression and misdirected ruler ship? Every round goes higher and higher – I am not the same woman I was 20 years ago, not even the same woman I was 1 year ago. In so doing I am learning to trust myself again and trust the Universe within me again. Some times it may have seemed as if I am in conflict with or turning my back on everything. This is far from the truth. The only thing that I turned my back on was the multiplied sorrow, the oppression and misguided control and ruler ship.

The planet, earth, humanity is looking for balance. It is looking for a harmonic that balances all of our selves. When allowing myself to be locked in a particular evolution by frequency or energy manipulation, (even unconsciously), I can only broadcast a similar frequency.

One of the main keys in finding this cooperation within oneself, this happy medium, is to become sovereign. You will need to have a space around you within which you can cooperate without feeling obligated to some one else. At the same time you cannot make demands on some one else without allowing them the same right. You will be redefining in many ways the whole concept of relationship and cooperation. Relationship is cooperation.

It is agreed cooperation of frequency / energy / vibration. Many of my old ways of relating were becoming very irritating because I was in the process of discovering a freedom frequency. Ideally, I had to learn how to be free while still being involved in an intricate number of relationships, while relating and relaying of a new life. I redefined the idea of femaleness and strength that felt good to me.

I did not have a pantheon of powerful female creator images. I had nothing on which to pattern a positive image of the empowered feminine. I was striving to be empowered through a male vibration because I did not have a clear vision of an empowered female. I realized I must create it. I must begin to recognize the wealth of energy in the new version of myself.

I became my own role model. Committing to loving myself and making this my number one step from which I operated, allowed every day and everything to fall into place. I started feeling more whole and complete.

This is not to say that we should return to the earlier female representations of the divine. However, what does remain true is that the energy frequency of the mind appears to be essentially male. The mind resists, fights for control, uses, manipulates, attacks, tries to grasp and possess and so on. This is why the traditional God is a patriarchal, controlling authority figure, an often-angry man you should live in fear of, as the Old Testament suggests. This God is the projection of the human mind.

To go beyond the mind and reconnect with the deeper reality of, I am that I am, very different qualities are needed: surrender, nonjudgmental, an openness to life that allows life to be instead of resisting it, the capacity to hold all tings in the loving embrace of your knowing. All of these qualities are much more closely related to the female energy. Whereas mind-energy is hard and rigid, being energy is soft and yielding and yet more powerful than the mind. The mind runs our civilization, being is in charge of all life on the planet and beyond. Being is the very intelligence whose visible manifestation is the physical universe.

I began regaining the function that is my birthright and therefore comes to me naturally: to be a bridge between the manifested world and the unmanifested, between the physical and spiritual.

There is a room. The room is in a house. The house is in a neighborhood. The neighborhood is in a city. The city is in a country. The country is on a continent. The continent is in a world. The world is on a planet and so on and so on. My viewpoint took this route from the bedroom to the Universe.

The Woman of Old

When she wished her virtues to shine throughout the land,

First she had to govern her state well, to govern her state well,

She had to establish harmony in her family. To establish harmony in her family, She had to discipline herself, to discipline herself,

She first had to set her mind in order... To set her mind in order, she first had to make her purpose sincere, To make her purpose sincere, She first had to extend her knowledge to the utmost... Such knowledge is acquired through a careful investigation of All things, For with all things investigated, knowledge becomes complete, With knowledge complete, the purpose becomes sincere,

With the purpose sincere, the mind is set in order... With the mind set in order there is real self-discipline, with real self-

discipline the family achieves harmony, with harmony in the family, the state becomes well governed... With the state well governed, there is peace throughout the land.

(I believe this was written by my personal mentor Nasik Shaleak)

Note to Self...

I am writing to you to affirm, confirm, and express the "you" that I know you are. You are amazing! You raised 11 children by yourself and never wavered, never gave up, never gave into letting go because it would have been easier. No one knows how hard you have worked, how hard it was to organize everything, how hard it was to maintain order, discipline, and faith in order that 11 individual souls could become the awesome souls they are today in spite of all of the impossibilities.

In spite of all of the impossibilities you still managed to study, learn, and maintain your intellect. Your ability to absorb knowledge is phenomenal. In spite of all of the impossibilities you still managed to remain kind, giving, generous and made a vow that nothing and no one would change your character, who you really are with in. You made a vow that the world would not give you a hard heart. You vowed that people would not take away your generosity. You vowed that when you do something / anything you would do it right and do it efficiently.

Inspite of all of the impossibilities you still managed to allow your gifts to flow through you. You still allowed yourself to evolve within these gifts. You endured what needed to be endured in order for you to continuously become more and more complete so that one day you could look in the mirror and be able to say, "I REALLY LIKE YOU"!

You are brave, never wavering in the face of challenges, obstacles, or your fears. Knowing that even if at any given moment you were not able or ready to face something, it would come back around and you would look whatever it was in the eye and say, "DO YOUR WORST", and you dealt with it and moved on.

So many times you have endured the excruciating soul wrenching pain of your children not understanding why you did what you did, blaming you for their pain, misery and anger. And after you laid on the floor curled up in a fetal position writhing in pain with the knowledge that you caused your child pain, you got up, took a deep breath owned it and moved forward and as a result have a better relationship with your children.

You are strong.... your life has been so impossibly difficult and challenging, (mentally, physically, emotionally, & spiritually), but you waded through whatever shit came at you with the knowledge and understanding that "EVEN SHIT MAKES GOOD FERTILIZER AND YOU CAN GROW NICE THINGS". Your capacity to love is immense. You love people, children, animals, nature, strangers, food, a good movie, the weather, etc., with passion, and you only ask that you be loved in return.

You speak 3 languages and can read and write 2 other languages. How cool is that? There is nothing you can't do. The world is your oyster and the sky is the limit. Even when you may forget sometimes, you still come back around to this thought process and you keep dreaming, you keep hoping, you keep visualizing the life that you desire. You have never given up on your dreams and desires even when for the time being they only exist in your mind. You truly are the "shizzle my nizzle"

THUNDEROUSLY WHISPERING

Talk to me thunderously whispering, The echo of freedom calling to my soul, Attaching itself to the ever evolving spirit Of what is holy within me.

Cry with me silently welcoming, The torrential waters reaching for my heart, Cleaving to the unlimited space, Of what was once emptiness embedded upon me.

O, but for the yearning of wisdom's pedigree, Groomed and prepared as a bride, Pending, longing for the moment which pulsates, In expectation of this next phase of life.

Walk with me carefully pondering, the intimacy of dreams entranced to my world, of different realities ever enshrined amongst the temple of our true being.

Approach with me ultimately uniting, the various realms of gods within, Upon which our sanctification Belies the sacredness of eternity.

O, but for the necessity of understanding's domain, Brought forth

on the wings of destiny

12/31/2026

Yesi...

So appreciate you on this journey!!! I feel so blessed to spend this time with you going into 2021... New journeys... new paths... new pages.

I truly hope that my words are as motivational & inspirational as you are to me.

♡ Lljane

Made in the USA
Columbia, SC
07 October 2020